We Weep for Ourselves and Our Children

We Weep for Ourselves and Our Children

A *Christian Guide for Survivors of Childhood Sexual Abuse*

Joanne Ross Feldmeth *and*
Midge Wallace Finley

 HarperSanFrancisco
A Division of HarperCollins*Publishers*

Part of the proceeds from this book will be contributed to:
VIRTUES, Inc. Foundation.

Unless otherwise noted, Scripture quotations in this publication are from the Holy Bible, New International Version. Copyright © 1973, 1978, 1984 International Bible Society. Used by permission of Zondervan Bible Publishers.

FIRST EDITION

Library of Congress Cataloging-in-Publication Data

Feldmeth, Joanne Ross.
    We weep for ourselves and our children : a Christian guide for survivors of childhood sexual abuse / Joanne Ross Feldmeth and Midge Wallace Finley.
        p.   cm.
    ISBN 0-06-062348-9
    1. Adult child abuse victims—Pastoral counseling of.   2. Incest victims—Pastoral counseling of.   3. Incest victims—Religious life.
    4. Adult child abuse victims—Religious life.   I. Finley, Midge Wallace.   II. Title.
        BV4463.5.F44   1990
        362.7'6—dc20   89-46446
                                                                        CIP

90 91 92 93 94 MCN 10 9 8 7 6 5 4 3 2 1

This edition is printed on acid-free paper that meets the American National Standards Institute Z39.48 Standards.

A large number of people followed him,
including women who mourned and wailed for him.

Jesus turned and said to them,
"Daughters of Jerusalem,
do not weep for me;
weep for yourselves
and for your children. . . .
for if men do these things
when the tree is green,
what will happen when it is dry?"

LUKE 23:27, 28, 31

CONTENTS

ACKNOWLEDGMENTS

This book is the product of many loving and supportive communities. Behind every writer working alone at her computer is a family willing to lose her for hours and days at a time! My husband Nate and my daughters Heather and Lindsay loved me and cheered me on through even the most difficult moments of this project. When Nate travelled and I was facing deadlines, my parents, Kenneth and Frances Ross, willingly gave up weekends to cook, chauffeur, and generally keep the household on track. Without the practical support of these five people, the book would still be sitting in pieces on my desk!

In the area of child sexual abuse treatment and education, I have had the great privilege of learning from leading experts in the field. Co-authoring a clinicians' study guide on child sexual abuse with Kee MacFarlane, M.S.W., was an incredible opportunity to learn how the recovery process begins for very young children. During this period I also met monthly with an excellent small discussion group on child abuse and ritual issues that was led by psychiatrist Roland Summit. These thought-provoking discussions were the beginning of my research on chapter 8.

Working at Children's Institute International provided

an invaluable education. Astrid Heger, M.D.—a pioneer in the medical diagnosis of child sexual abuse—has been a good friend whose dedication to children and spiritual commitment continue to inspire me. Toni Cavanagh Johnson, Ph.D., provided state-of-the-art information on her work with children who molest other children.

Through the Southern California Training Center for Child Sexual Abuse Treatment, I was able to benefit from lectures, seminars and informative discussions with staff members and invited experts. It was a special privilege to work with Training Center Director Esther Gillies, L.C.S.W. and Assistant Directors Joe Palacios, M.F.C.C., and Linda Russell, L.C.S.W. It was also very helpful to have access to the Marshall Resource Center's collection on child sexual abuse treatment.

Carmen Berry, M.S.W., the author of *When Helping You Is Hurting Me* (Harper & Row, 1988) was this project's tireless "advocate." She believed in the book's message and she consistently encouraged me to reframe my professional commitments so that I had time for myself and for writing. I have been profoundly affected by her book, her friendship, and her example.

My coauthor, Midge Wallace Finley, M.F.C.C., has taught me much about the power of relationships and support groups in recovery. I am grateful for her partnership on this journey. Through Midge, I also gained the editorial insight, friendship, and prayer support of Sue Konkel, M.A., Ellen Rivera, and Cindy Wygal. Dr. Win Griffin, M.F.C.C., helped me move from a theoretical grasp to a personal understanding of Inner Child issues. Also, a word of special appreciation goes to our editor, Rebecca Laird, whose commitment to this project and patience with its authors lasted throughout the four years it took to get from concept to completion.

For three of those years, I have also had a remarkable relationship with a group we call the "Southwest Seven": a therapist, an English professor, an actress/director, a writer, a social ethicist, a railroad conductor, and a feminist historian. A series of discussions on "Women and Power" became a group friendship which has outlasted members' job changes, family changes, graduations, and out-of-state moves. Thanks to Sharon Billings, M.F.C.C., Anne Eggebroten, Ph.D., Barbara Graber, M.A., Loie Lorenzen, Ph.D., Jeanne Sales, and Karen Torjesen, Ph.D., I know about the joy and power of support groups first hand.

Finally, I must say that although I am not an incest victim, this project forced me to confront a spiritual crisis of my own. My faith was challenged and ultimately strengthened as I searched the words of Jesus, the prayers of Job, and the tradition of professional women mourners to find a biblical model that fit the recovery process Christian survivors described to me. The lessons I learned brought about a profound inner change and a new commitment to the God who grieves with us.

Joanne Ross Feldmeth
March, 1990

I am deeply grateful that God provided me not only with the opportunity to grow and stretch spiritually and professionally through this project, but with a number of healing relationships to support me throughout the process. I especially wish to acknowledge my gratitude to:

My four children: Karen, Patty, Terri and Mike—for allowing me to be who I really am (besides their mom!).

Caring friends: Barbara Anderson, Jan Allebrand, Marsi Beauchamp, Sue Konkel, Kathy Bertrand, Joann Young, Judy Stewart, Jean Luther, Cindy Wygal, Ellen Rivera, and Leslie Byers, who were a constant source of support, encouragement and honesty.

Support Groups: VIRTUES Leadership Team—awesome women whose commitment to help themselves and others to heal inspired me to persevere.

First Evangelical Free Church in Fullerton, California

Divorce Recovery Team—my surrogate family, where I always feel a sense of belonging

The Deacon Board—a caring community within the Body of Christ

My co-author: Joanne Ross Feldmeth, for her gift of writing and her determination to tell real stories of hope and recovery.

Our editor: Rebecca Laird, who never stopped believing in this project.

Valued colleagues and friends: Especially generous with their gifts were:
Dr. Earl Henslin
Dr. Bethyl Shepperson
Jeanne Yorke, M.F.C.C.
Pastor Buck Buchanan

Special thanks: To Dr. Joyce Hulgus, who became my "surrogate mom" and created a "holding environment" as I peeled away layers of my own life and revealed a very hurting inner child who needed healing from past relationships. Her valuable input into emotional and spiritual healing through relationships has added much depth to my life and to this work.

My prayer for any survivor who reads this book is that you will no longer be bound by the acts of others against you, but that the TRUTH will free you to build a relationship with a loving and personal GOD, who gives dignity and worth to all, through His Son, Jesus Christ.

Midge Wallace Finley
March, 1990

PROLOGUE

The group is gathered in a simple church room usually used for Sunday School classes. There are hymnals and Bibles stacked on the corner piano. In the center of the room, metal chairs (the folding type with only the barest padding) form a lopsided circle. It is the group's first meeting and as the women take their places, only a few whispered conversations break the uneasy silence. The group of nine includes a support group leader, a coleader, and seven group members. Later, as the members introduce themselves, one woman blurts out, "Oh, you all look so *normal*," and the room explodes in nervous laughter.

Most of the group members have never met before but they have one thing in common: they were all sexually abused as children. The support group leader explains that the group "rules" are simple. There is no charge for attending the group, but members are asked to commit themselves to attending all ten sessions. The group's purpose is support, not therapy, but members are asked to attend individual therapy sessions with a therapist of their own choice during the three-month term.

Briefly, the leader explains that the group's primary task is to share stories that members have seldom dared to tell before. Every story is to be listened to with acceptance and love. Every group member, however, has the right to decide when—and if—she wants to talk. The coleader notes, "Since sexually abused children must repress their real feelings in order to protect grown-ups, it is important that in this group, real feelings—including negative feelings—can be expressed openly. When people have been physically, emotionally, and spiritually betrayed, they have a lot of despair and anger. Some of their rage will be directed at their families; some of it will be directed at God. This group is here to listen even to the most painful feelings. It is a type of grief work that can only be done in supportive communities."

When the leaders finish, the group members introduce themselves:

Kate is a 29-year-old single woman who works as a bank manager. She says that she has been in therapy for over a year, but "The only group I've ever belonged to was a diet group, and," she adds with a grin, "I couldn't stand it!"

Connie is a 32-year-old single graduate student in theology. "I've been in therapy and a support group for over two years. There are times when it has kept me alive."

Donna is a tiny redhead with a nervous smile. "I'm 35, I have one daughter, and I have the distinction of being the first divorced person in my family. I'm here mainly because my therapist suggested it. The truth is, well, I'm not sure I was really sexually abused. If my family knew I was here tonight, they'd be furious."

Alice is 51 and has been in therapy "off and on" for six years. She has been married for twenty-eight years and has three grown children. "I am so glad to be in a support group led by Christians," she says brightly.

Sharon, a 44-year-old blonde, shakes her head at Alice's comment. "You know, I have mixed feelings about that. I've spent about ten years working with a couple of good therapists but I haven't found very many Christians I can talk to honestly about my childhood. My father was a Christian and he molested me. My first husband was a minister and he had affairs. My best friend was a Christian counselor and he molested my son. Sometimes I feel like I'm hanging on to my faith by my fingernails."

Gerri grins at Sharon and says, "Cheer up. I'm hanging onto my *sanity* by my fingernails—and (holding up the hands of a veteran nailbiter), there isn't much to hang on with! I'm 37 years old, I have two kids, and I'm still married, although the marriage isn't great. After years of not having any memory of *anything* before I was about 12, memories of my childhood—and of being sexually abused—started flooding back eighteen months ago. The memories are scary. My parents were into some pretty heavy stuff, including prostitution and the occult. I was in the hospital for a while and I'm still in individual and group therapy."

Ruth says softly, "All of this talk about years in therapy makes me a little nervous because I've had exactly one session. Also, the pastor at our church is very leery of psychology. I am going to therapy, frankly, because it is a requirement to join this group.

"Unlike Gerri, I've never forgotten my childhood—I just wish I could. I'm 45 this month and I have four children: two boys and two girls. My oldest daughter just turned 13, which is the age I was when my uncle started to molest me. It went on for years and my parents did nothing. But the thing is, I look at my daughter Sandy and I am just enraged at her. I know that is crazy, but that is what I feel. I cannot stand to have the girl in the room with me. I'm hoping that this group and the therapist can help me—I don't want to hate my own child."

The leader thanks them for coming and tells them that next week, they will begin sharing stories of their childhoods. She explains that sharing these stories can create an almost magical bond, for while they are very different people, they will see their own lives and secret losses reflected in every other story told.

The chapters that follow belong to these women and their stories, and to the power of their truth. All names and many significant life details have been changed to protect identities, and most of the characters are composites based on more than one person. The group the book follows is fictional, although the group's interaction is based on numerous real experiences with support groups.

This book's emphasis on integrating emotional and spiritual healing is a response to the frustrations we heard expressed by Christian survivors. Consistently, these women told us: "My pastor tells me to forgive and forget—but I can't!" "I can't pray," "People at my church refuse to listen to my anger or my pain," "Talking about God the Father scares me" or "Going to church makes me feel isolated and confused." Yet, surprisingly, the same survivors seemed absolutely committed to their personal faith.

As we listened to these women, we realized that they

had suffered spiritual as well as emotional trauma. They wanted—and deserved—support in seeking a recovery that did not close off either their emotional or spiritual growth. For both of us as authors, our conviction grew out of several years involvement in some aspect of child abuse treatment or research.

Joanne Feldmeth has served as Director of Communications at Children's Institute International (CII), and is currently Educational Resources Coordinator at CII's Southern California Training Center on Child Sexual Abuse Treatment. She is the author of numerous articles on recovery issues and the booklet *Why Good Kids Make Good Victims* (Arcadia, CA: Focus on the Family, 1985). She is coauthor of *Response/Child Sexual Abuse: The Clinical Interview* (New York: Guilford Press, 1988) and *A Straight Word to Kids and Their Parents* (Rifton, NY: Plough Publishing House, 1987). Her work on integrating the emotional and spiritual issues in sexual abuse began with a 1984 magazine assignment to write an article on incest in Christian homes.

Midge Finley's work as a licensed Marriage, Family and Child Counselor in Fullerton, California, has included extensive experiences with individual and group therapy for adult survivors, although none of the characters in the book are based on her private clients. The book's emphasis on the healing power of community is a direct reflection of her clinical experience and ministry. After four years of support group work, Midge and a group of Christian survivors founded the VIRTUES (Victims of Incest Recover Through Understanding, Education, and Support) network in September of 1987. VIRTUES is a model support group system which can be replicated in a variety of church and para-church settings. At present, VIRTUES chapters have been started in churches representing six different denominational groups. The program includes professional supervision, leaders groups, survivors groups, and annual retreats. VIRTUES affiliated groups have also been offered for husbands and mothers of child sexual abuse survivors.

A word should be said about the book's exclusive focus on women and particularly, the use of the pronoun "she" when we are discussing the survivor. The myth that boys are seldom the victims of child sexual abuse is rapidly being discredited by research. Most of the survivors we had contact with, however, were women and all of the survivor support groups Midge organized were exclusively female. Support groups for adult male survivors are beginning to be offered (including a planned affiliate program of VIRTUES); however, most are still in the pioneering stage. While we suspect that adult male survivors will find that their emotional and spiritual problems are similar to the women whose stories we have included, we did not have the data to generalize about the male experience.

Adult survivor support groups for women, on the other hand, are well established. Over 300 women have been involved in church based support groups, retreats, and leaders groups which Midge has led or coordinated since 1984. Almost fifty group members filled out and returned to us surveys on their support group experience and emotional and spiritual issues in incest recovery. We also talked to numerous survivors who had pursued recovery in secular self-help groups, group therapy, and/or individual therapy. In addition, Joanne interviewed over twenty-five experts in various aspects of child abuse, including psychologists, child development specialists, social workers, government agency administrators, and law enforcement officers. Eventually, we selected a dozen survivors with whom we conducted interviews over a period of three years. These women are the basis of the seven characters in the book. Each of them reported a multilevel grieving process that was complex and compelling. They reminded us of the "women skilled in mourning"[1] that the prophet Jeremiah once asked to weep for Israel's broken dreams. At odds with an American church that too often sees faith as a talisman to ward off suffering, these women used honest grief as a spiritual tool to face the very real injustices of life. Far from being joyless and dour, the women engaged in this process struck us as exceptionally alive. They shook with laughter as well as tears as they shared their feelings and their lives.

On a personal, social, and spiritual level, they mourned the losses in their childhoods and recovered the Inner Child once hidden and isolated within them. These women not only gave us permission to include them in the book, but became a special support group for the project, often volunteering their journals, poetry, drawings, and prayers. The stories they told us in individual interviews and some special group sessions are filled with truths that apply to anyone who needs to grieve and recover from the hurts of the past.

We Weep for Ourselves and Our Children

Chapter 1

DISCOVERY OF THE LOST CHILD

"Pretty, aren't they?" Kate said, tapping the delicate cup and saucer. "These two settings are all I have left of the original twelve. It was a huge set: turkey platters, bowls, butter dishes, salt and pepper shakers, plates, soup bowls, the works. I broke every other piece—one at a time—against that kitchen wall."

Fingering the cup lightly, she talked about a long weekend years ago when her childhood memories of being sexually assaulted by her uncle drove her to despair and grief. The only relief from the overpowering feelings came from her tears and the sound of the china shattering.

As the pile of broken dishes on the kitchen floor grew, it formed, in an odd way, a memorial to the little girl who had been hurt by someone she trusted. Kate was finally paying attention to the inner wound that everyone else had ignored.

After two days of grieving, she put the remaining few dishes in her cupboard. "I often use this china when I am having someone over; there is just enough left for the two of us to have coffee and cookies. If she seems troubled, I tell her about the dishes." Sometimes, Kate discovers that her guest was also sexually victimized as a child.

Kate's systematic destruction of her china set is a type of grieving ritual that seems eccentric only in the context of today's Western society. Most world cultures have carefully constructed ceremonies that give outward expression to life's great changes and losses. Modern Western society has taken away most of those rites—but not our need to express our losses. We are left—like Kate—to create our own rituals.

The Price of Silence

For the Princess Tamar, an incest victim whose story is recorded in the Bible, there was a cultural model for grieving. Raped by her half-brother Amnon and then brutally rejected, she tore her ornate robes and rubbed ashes in her hair, following the custom of her people. When her brother Absalom met the sobbing teenager, however, he could not tolerate her grieving. Instead, he advised, "Be quiet now, my sister; he is your brother. Don't take this thing to heart."

If Tamar's ritual seems primitive and foreign, her brother's words are painfully familiar to people who were sexually abused as children. If the child molester is a family member or friend (and overwhelmingly, perpetrators fall into that category), the adults in the child's life will strive to protect the family reputation and minimize the importance of the sexual abuse. "Keep quiet . . . don't take this thing to heart," they suggest. Like Absalom, they believe that keeping quiet, trying to forget and denying the damage, will stop the pain. It does not. The secrecy draws a tight ring of isolation around the wounded person, and allows an unhealthy family system to flourish. The passage in 2 Samuel 13 notes that once silenced, Tamar "lived in her brother Absalom's house, a desolate woman." Her father, the great King David, never attempted to comfort her or to punish Amnon. Refusing to publicly acknowledge the truth about what had happened, he simply allowed Tamar to be shut away.

Absalom, stung by his brother's crime and his father's silence, murdered Amnon and launched a campaign to steal David's throne. During this attempted coup, Absalom raped 10 women in David's harem. Sexual assault of the king's wives was political and moral treachery. It required that he treat these women— members of his family—with the same contempt his brother had showed Tamar. Absalom the avenger became Absalom the rapist, Absalom the incest perpetrator.

Eventually his coup failed, and he was killed by his father's supporters. Before he died, however, Absalom fathered a beautiful daughter and named her Tamar. David's family is a classic case study of dysfunction and sexual abuse, of the power of unacknowledged pain to reenact itself again and again.

Kate's family was caught in this same pattern of reenacting unacknowledged pain. As teenagers, Kate's mother Edith and her mothers two cousins had been molested by Edith's stepbrother, Charles. Yet when Kate was just 2—and again when she was 4 years old— Edith dropped her off at Uncle Charles's house for a two week visit. Kate shook her head, remembering, "She dressed me up in my very best dress. . . .

"Years later, when I was 28 and hadn't spoken to her

for months, I met my mother for lunch. I told her that with my therapist I had painfully pieced together very early memories of being raped by Uncle Charles.

"She looked at me oddly and asked, 'Are you sure?' "

"Yes, I'm sure," I told her.

"Then she poured herself a cup of tea and said, 'Well I'm sure it wasn't as bad as what I had to put up with from him!' "

Minimizing the Pain

Like Kate, other survivors of child sexual abuse have often found that if they break through the wall of secrecy to tell someone about their past, their pain is either denied outright or minimized as unimportant and unworthy of attention. One survivor waited more than twenty years to tell her pastor of a childhood marred by her father's sexual abuse. "Well, that happened a long time ago, didn't it?" he asked, coolly. "Why don't you just forget it?"

When they grow up, children who have had experiences of sexual abuse often try to minimize the impact just as their family and society have done. It is typical for survivors to spend a lot of energy suppressing memories of explaining why their experience is unimportant. The following comments are representative:

"You know, my grandfather didn't go all the way with me—so it wasn't that bad."

"It only happened a couple times."

"My stepdad used to try sexual stuff with my sister—but he left me alone."

"My mom used to pull me into closets and rub against

me after the divorce. It was weird, but she didn't really do anything."

"My babysitter used to try to touch us and he always tried to stand where he could watch us undress but nothing really happened."

The truth is that these statements are exercises in self-delusion. Something significant did happen. An adult who is sexual or seductive toward a child will create deep hurt and confusion that can have a lifelong impact on the child's sense of self, whether or not intercourse occurs. There is an effect on a child even when it is her sister or brother who is the direct object of the adult's sexual acting out.

In addition to minimizing and denying the impact of the sexual abuse, many survivors bury traumatic incidents—or even whole sections of their childhood—deep within the unconscious. If a survivor manages to break through the "keep quiet" messages around her, however, she runs a real risk of being blamed for the abuse.

Blaming the Victim

"I saw Uncle Charles again when I was in eighth grade, and I was terrified of him without knowing why," Kate remembered. "But even if I had consciously recalled those memories of his abuse, I would have known better than to mention them to my family.

"Just the year before, my foster sister had become engaged to the very eligible 27-year-old music minister at our church. My parents were thrilled with her 'catch.' I was just as dazzled by Matt as they were. He had started a popular youth choir and he was often a featured soloist at church services. I was thrilled when he would take time to talk to me, a shy junior-higher. He spent a lot of time at our house, even when my sister was not home. I was flattered that during those times he would seek me out, flustered but pleased by his hugs and kisses. This was the big brother I had always wanted.

"It is hard to believe how naive I really was; how needy, I suppose, to have some attention. Eventually, however, it was clear that Matt was doing things that went far beyond anything even I could interpret as a brother's affection. I tried to avoid him, but it didn't work. I think he knew I didn't have enough of a sense of self to say no in any effectual way. I just mumbled and tried to leave. When he was insistent—and angry—I just stiffened and left emotionally. That ability—to disassociate—was one I had learned well. 'Be quiet, pretend it isn't happening,' I told myself.

"By now, Matt knew that I wouldn't give him any trouble. He became more of a bully when we were together, and eventually insisted on intercourse with me. Later, when I cried, he sneered, 'Oh shut up, you wanted it too.' That shocked me. I didn't much know what I wanted, but I was sure I hadn't wanted this.

"Finally, stuttering and stumbling, I tried to tell my family that Matt 'tried things' with me when we were alone. They stared at me—a very plump adolescent gazing in terror from behind thick glasses—and laughed. I heard their laughter for years, I think. I can still feel the heat behind my eyes and the blush stealing across my face as my mother said, 'You're just trying to get attention!'

"My father refused to discuss it at all, and my foster sister was furious with me for trying to 'steal' her boyfriend. Three months later, she married Matt at a huge church wedding.

"My mother, however, did have one last word on the topic. Drawing me aside at the wedding, she said grimly, 'If anything really *did* happen, you can't wear white when you marry and you can never marry a minister like Matt!'

"After that, I stopped going to church."

The Work of Mourning

"For the next few years, all I thought about was leaving home. I got a job right after high school and moved out. I never had trouble finding work, but I had constant problems with relationships. I was naive; I had not been raised to take care of myself. I got used a lot.

"After several years on my own, I started to notice that my memory had huge gaps. I was in my mid 20's before I realized that other people remembered things while I had blocked out whole years of my life. I have report cards; that's how I know I went to school. All of that is repressed. I still run into people who say, 'We went to such-and-such a school together,' and I play along. I have only 'patches' of recollection, selective memories."

At 27, Kate reached the first of a series of inner crises: "All of my life, I had never slept well, but now the nightmares were getting more vivid and more frequent. One, which I had for fifteen years—sometimes every night for weeks on end—was about a skinless dog.

"In the dream, I lived alone because no one wanted to be near me. I was walking down the street when this dog came up to me and I realized that it had no skin. You know how encyclopedias show illustrations of bodies with plastic overlays for the organs and the arteries and so on? That was how this dog looked!

"The dog followed me home and I was filled with a horrible ambivalence. At least now I wasn't alone, but I was repelled by the dog's ugliness. I felt so sorry for it, however, that I fed it dinner and let it stay. To my horror, it curled up next to me on the bed and would not move. I knew then that it would be with me for the rest of my life, and I wanted to die. Instead, however, I fell into a deep sleep.

"The next morning, I awoke nine months pregnant and in labor. I went to the hospital and brought the dog with me. But when the doctor delivered my baby, he yelled, 'Kill it! Kill it! Look at that!' And I looked and the baby was just like the dog—it had no skin.

"I usually awoke screaming.

"I became afraid of dogs, pregnant women, babies, and most of all, of getting close to people. The urge for suicide was increasing. I really had no idea why I was so full of panic. I thought it was some hidden insanity. By then, I was attending church again and I couldn't understand why going to services made me so upset.

"I got into therapy, and I spent hours and hours crying in anticipation. Even after four months in treatment, I did not know what was upsetting me. In May, I gave myself just six months to find out what was going on inside or I decided I would commit suicide. I was at the end of my rope. I cried out to God, 'Show me where all this pain is coming from!'

"Nothing changed right away. Then on June 1, I woke up with tremendous apprehension and the memories started. Anything, everything triggered memories I had repressed. I filled the sink with water and suddenly was sobbing, remembering a childhood Christmas.

"I came home every night for days and would sit on the kitchen floor and feel. I cried. I realized I had never really been able to relate to anyone; I had faked it. I spent hours staring at the ceiling fan in my bedroom. I couldn't eat. I took sick leave from work, and when I did go in I was useless.

"Then in August, I was driving down the street when the memories of the rape came back: the sounds, the shadow on the wallpaper, the sensations, the look on my uncle's face. For the first time in years, I remembered. It hit me at that moment that my parents had known about my uncle molesting other children and still had not protected me. All my life I had been a 'skinless baby'—no boundaries, no protection. That was when I decided I had to break something. The anger, the anguish, just had to go somewhere.

"Actually, I wanted to destroy my antique china cabinet. My therapist kept suggesting all these floppy, therapeutic toys. I told her, 'Get serious! We're talking about someone raping a child!' Kate said, grinning in spite of herself. "We compromised on the dishes.

"After the three days of breaking dishes, I made myself a cup of coffee and poured it in a remaining cup and just sat and looked at the pile of china. I had cried until there were no tears left, but I had a sense of tremendous relief."

Loss of the Inner Self

Alice Miller has written that "not to have been loved just as one truly was" is probably the greatest of personal wounds, and it "cannot heal without the work of mourning."[1] At long last, Kate was acknowledging and mourning the pain of her past. Her grief was for a child who had been left and lost: the inner self who had remained traumatized not only by sexual abuse as a preschooler and an adolescent but also by years of family betrayal and abandonment.

Just as her family had reacted to her suffering not with shared grieving and comfort but with denial and blame, Kate reacted to her pain by self-hatred and rejection of her own memories. Blocked from her own experiences and feelings, she had no foundation for an authentic sense of self. The only part of her that felt real was the shame.

Recent studies document that people who were sexually abused as children suffer a long-term loss of self-esteem.[2] Obviously, people vary in their reactions, but the blow to the identity is consistent and serious. This childhood trauma attacks the sense of self at a critical point—before it has finished the important work of growing up. Understanding how the sense of self is originally formed—and how it is derailed by the crisis of abuse—shows the need for a multilevel recovery process. [3]

As authors we have combined elements from several models of building or rebuilding self-esteem[3] to reflect the primary issues that repeatedly come up in individual and group discussions with survivors of incest.[2] Briefly, here is an outline of how these "building blocks" establish positive self-esteem:

1. *Virtue or spiritual value:* A child who perceives from the way she is treated that she has spiritual or

intrinsic worth believes "I am good (even if I sometimes make mistakes or do bad things)," and "I am valuable." This is a child who does not do good things in order to earn value, but whose accomplishments flow from an inner belief in her spiritual worth.

2. *Connectedness and community.* Developmentally, an infant is "we"—merged in identity with Mother—before she or he can become "I." Established early in our interactions with family, our relationships remain a critical part of our personal identity throughout life. This is the part of the identity that proclaims, "I am loved. I am part of—and can trust—a group beyond myself."

3. *Sexuality and gender identity:* Emotional development is closely linked to the healthy emergence of the child's sexuality and gender identity, as the child matures through a series of stages from infancy through adolescence. One of the first things children learn about themselves is "I am a girl" or "I am a boy." We talk to, respond to, and hold children differently depending on their gender. The differences may not be as significant as the overall sense that being a girl—or being a boy—is a positive, valuable identity.

4. *Power:* This part of the self develops with the child's growing knowledge that "I can make choices. I can take action." The choices she makes as well as the power she feels give the child new clues about who she is and what she can do. Even the limits to that power—the legitimate boundaries

of her life—teach her something about her identity. If she emerges with a positive but realistic sense of her power, her self-esteem will be high.

The development of a healthy self can be stunted by damage to any of these four areas. In the case of sexual abuse, however, *all of these connectors of self-esteem are fractured.* David Finkelhor has identified four traumatizing factors[4] that directly undermine and stunt these foundational building blocks of a child's identity. They are as follows:

1. *Stigmatization:* The abuser's actions are painful evidence that the child is not valued or respected. Even very young children understand that sexual abuse is a shameful secret, and this stigma profoundly alters the child's sense of virtue or inner worthiness. The "don't tell" message (whether a spoken threat or not) keeps the child isolated in her feelings of shame.

2. *Betrayal:* Double-crossed by someone older and trusted, the child has her belief in connections shattered. If she is unsupported by those closest to her, the child loses her family emotionally. The message "don't trust" will seem accurate and appropriate since her deepest pain is associated with her most intimate and trusted connections.

3. *Traumatic sexualization:* Children are not ready emotionally or physically for sexual relationships, and a molestation traumatizes the natural process that links physical stages, emotional development, and the emergence of healthy sexuality. Feeling good about being a girl or a boy and enjoying

sexuality as a healthy part of the self becomes extremely difficult. Sexual reactions to abuse can vary enormously, from rejecting and repressing all sexual feelings within the self to seeing the self only in sexual terms, as a sex object. Whether the child splits off from emotional or physical connections to her sexuality, the message to the Inner Child is clear: "Don't feel!"

4. *Powerlessness:* Children cannot control sexual relationships with adults. The older person holds the power and—whether the child resists or cooperates—the relationship is built on the adult's needs and decisions, not the child's. Sexual abuse profoundly alters the child's view of her own ability to control not only circumstances, but also her own body. On the one hand, she may have an unrealistic belief that she could have stopped the sexual encounters with an older, more powerful person. On the other hand, the survivor of a dysfunctional family seldom has much life experience in making any kind of meaningful personal choices. The message of her family was "You don't *have* choices," or even more threatening, "Don't say no to me!"

Three of the four messages that we have linked to the traumatizing factors of child sexual abuse ("Don't tell"; "Don't trust"; "Don't feel") have been associated with the alcoholic family.[5] In fact, all dysfunctional families tend to have a belief system that includes these tenets. It is also important to note that all four of the traumatizing factors isolated by Finkelhor are present in other life experiences. Adult date rape, for example, has the same

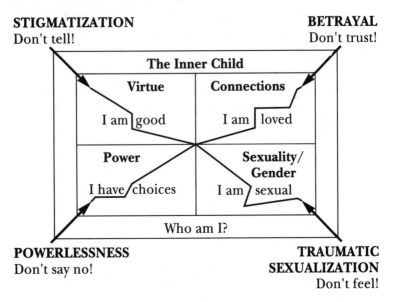

STIGMATIZATION
Don't tell!

BETRAYAL
Don't trust!

POWERLESSNESS
Don't say no!

**TRAUMATIC
SEXUALIZATION**
Don't feel!

Figure 1. Child Sexual Abuse: The Attack on the Inner Child

elements and is also a formidable attack on the survivor's self-esteem. *The difference in child sexual abuse is the enormous significance of developmental timing.* Children and adolescents are still in the beginning stages of building a sense of self.

If an abused child is isolated from people who can support her grieving process and reframe and balance this experience, the child's inner identity is compromised (see figure 1). Instead of building her identity around this shameful, hated, powerless, and sexually abused self, the child emotionally separates, splitting off from her now vulnerable (or "skinless") Inner Child. With the foundation for selfhood seriously damaged in childhood, the survivor can spend years erecting an imitation (often a magnificently convincing one) of an adult with an intact identity and self-esteem.

Repressing memories and the identity of the real, damaged self helps many survivors get through the minefield of life with an abusive family. In adulthood, however, these patterns are as destructive to the inner self as the original abuse. Denying the little-girl or little-boy feelings and memories within and boarding up the true self produces developmental stalemate and a "false self." While most people realize that they have a many-faceted self within, those who were badly hurt as children are blocked from a sense of wholeness and reconciliation.

Moreover, when they detect the cut-off feelings of their Inner Child (or real self) emerging, they panic. Their first reaction is to beat down or ignore this hated "foreigner" within.

Jesus and the Child

It is important to stress that it is not only the dysfunctional family but also society as a whole that shames and despises vulnerability and children and encourages us to hate our Inner Child. The messages children receive from school, the media, and even church to "act grown-up" imply that acting like a child (even during childhood) is unacceptable. Miller has written eloquently of the vested interest adults have in taking this attitude: "Contempt for those who are smaller and weaker . . . is the best defense against a breakthrough of one's own feelings of helplessness."[6]

The stories of Jesus, however, establish a view of children and childhood that is radically different from the one society reflects. When his disciples rebuked mothers for bothering Jesus by bringing children to him for a blessing, he remonstrated, "Let the little children come to me, and do not hinder them, for the kingdom of heaven belongs to such as these" (Matt. 19:14). Indeed, Jesus presented the child as an example of true spirituality:

He called a little child and had him stand among them. And he said: "I tell you the truth, unless you change and become like little children, you will never enter the kingdom of heaven. Therefore, whoever humbles himself like this child is the greatest in the kingdom of heaven. And whoever welcomes a little child like this in my name welcomes me." (Matt. 18:2–5a)

Those who, like Kate, begin to seek and welcome the little child within themselves, can take courage from the fact that they are on a spiritual journey.

Embracing the Inner Self

In Arthur Miller's play *After the Fall*, a character recounts a dream not unlike Kate's nightmare: "I dreamed I had a child and even in the dream, I saw it was my life, and it was an idiot and I ran away. But it always crept onto my lap again, clutched at my clothes until I thought, if I could kiss it, whatever in it was my own, perhaps I could sleep. And I bent to its broken face and it was horrible . . . but I kissed it; I think one must finally take one's life in one's own arms."[7]

This was the path Kate had begun to journey along. Maggie Scarf has written that mourning allows the person who was lost to be internalized.[8] For the victim of incest, the lost person is her own Inner Child, the little-girl feelings within. By taking her life in her arms and internalizing the very inner self she had lost and despised, Kate's healing had begun.

"At first, I completely resisted the idea of loving the little girl inside," Kate admitted. "I thought she was ugly, terrifying. She had haunted my dreams for years! Then I found a picture that helped me tremendously. It was a painting of a sleeping infant. She was on her tummy, one little hand out, her eyes shut. This picture reminded me of my unconscious self. So much of me was still asleep. All these years, I thought, no one loved that little child. So it became my job that year to learn to love her.

"At this point, I changed my name, dropping my family name, Murphy, and just used my first and middle names. I had new business cards made and eventually went through the legal channels to become Kate Rose."

To her delight, two friends sent her pink carnations and "Congratulations on Your New Baby Girl" cards. "Before I changed my name," Kate remembered, "I felt that the child was saying, 'I'm not ever, ever coming out.' But now, I was validating that child's existence. I had mourned a child who had died. Now, in a way, the child was being born again.

"I really did not know how to love myself at first. My therapist had me make a list of things I could do to nurture myself and one at a time, she supported me in accomplishing them over a six-month period. I grew up thinking I could not play with boys' toys, so at 29, I bought a pickup truck! I lost thirty pounds and got a new haircut. After years of being a polyester mouse in thick glasses, I bought a leather skirt and green-tinted contact lenses!

"It was great. I suggested to my therapist that I was ready to terminate treatment. For three months I felt 'cured.' Then I began to date a new man from church and within weeks, I was overwhelmed with the same crushing depression, insomnia, nightmares, returning memories.

"The anger I felt this time was that I had already 'fixed' the problem and here it was again!" Kate sighed, "I'm beginning to think that incest issues are like the layers of baklava. You peel off one layer, then you find another. A new memory, a new recovery."

Having embraced her Inner Child at one level, she was appalled at the extent of this skinless baby's neediness. Kate's impatience is typical of people recovering from childhood trauma, particularly child sexual abuse. Healing is a process of recovering a self that has not only been lost to consciousness but also has been actually stunted in its developmental process by the crisis of sexual molestation. There is no skipping over those stages of development. The instinctive response as each level is revealed, however, is to stuff the real feelings that emerge, and split from the helpless and vulnerable Inner Child. If a survivor stays isolated from others, she is particularly at risk for this response. "When we are left alone to mourn our losses," Louise Kaplan has noted, "Then splitting takes over."[9]

Recognizing that she could not mourn these tremendous inner losses alone, Kate joined a support group for survivors. A model for mourning that moves survivors beyond the stigma and isolation of sexual abuse to community is critical to recovery. For Kate and others damaged in childhood, it is difficult to accept the self before the self has been accepted by others. Grieving that allows the survivor to again embrace a community and move out of isolation can free the incest survivor from the cycle of self-blame, self-hatred, and self-destruction.

Chapter 2

THE SURVIVOR AND SHAME

"It just felt good to erase my name," Connie said quietly. "I wrote it and rubbed it out again and again. I wanted to disappear. I have always lived with that feeling but it was manageable until I came to California to attend seminary. Within the first few weeks, my car broke down. The oil light kept coming on, but I assumed there was a short in the light so I ignored it. The engine burned out and I couldn't afford to replace it. That was the beginning of something snapping inside. I was enraged and the anger was all directed at me. It was as if my mistake with my car proved that all the self-loathing I had felt for years was justified. I became intensely depressed and suicidal."

The timing of the car breakdown was especially difficult. Connie had just moved away from the Northwest, where she had a network of friends and a fulfilling job as part of a campus ministry organization. Deciding to come to seminary had meant a major financial investment, and there was no money in her budget for major car repairs. She asked her mother, a comparatively wealthy widow, for help with the bill and was turned down. "I wasn't surprised," Connie said, "But I didn't know who else to ask."

To be in Southern California without a car is, as

Connie noted, "like an amputation." Still, she quickly agreed that car trouble is not usually the precursor to suicidal depression. "It's me!" she said, shaking her head and grinning. "I always say that when other people are depressed, they get symptoms; when I'm depressed, my car breaks down." While the car sat useless in the driveway, Connie's depression darkened. She managed to attend seminary classes but panic attacks and suicidal thoughts were becoming chronic.

"I started going to therapy at that point. I thought I was going crazy. On the one hand, I was convinced that something had happened to me, something that explained my terror and shame," she remembered. "On the other hand, I had no clear memory of what that 'something' was. I told my therapist, 'I think my mom tried to drown me.' But while I could not get that thought out of my head, I had no memory of the incident.

"I also told him, 'Please, I have to know whether my dad molested me,'" she said. "Again, I had no specific memories but my dreams and my fears consistently centered on that issue. Finally, I asked for hypnosis because I felt that the cause for my enormous self-hatred was just under the surface."[1]

Retrieving Buried Memories

The first memory to emerge under hypnosis was, however, not about either of her parents nor about a forgotten incident. It was about a car. "I had always remembered the accident I had when I was 6," Connie said. "We were turning a corner onto a busy street and I went flying out of the car. Another car almost hit me. I remember coming to on a sofa, seeing nurses, bright lights, and bandages. But as I told my therapist about the memory under hypnosis, he asked very softly, 'Connie, did you open the door?' Without any hesitation, I said yes. Immediately, the feelings I had then came flooding back. Even then, I had wanted to die. I opened the car door because I couldn't see any other way out of my pain."

More repressed memories came back in the sessions that followed. Some were painfully vivid. "From the age of around 4 until I was 6," Connie explained, "my dad sexually abused me. The physical sensations of choking and chronic nausea returned with the memories of having oral sex forced on me. Perhaps the most difficult part of this was that my father was the only one of my parents to show any affection or interest in me. He was my only source of caring, and yet he had been so cruel. He hurt me and he must have known that I was hurt. He would stifle my cries with a pillow. It was a brutal betrayal."

When she was 6, Connie tried to tell her mother what her father was doing to her at night. "I was sitting in the bathtub at the time," Connie explained. "My mother became hysterical. She had her hands on my throat. She called me a liar and she screamed, 'You've always come between your father and me!' I thought she was going to drown me."

Not long after that, Connie jumped out of the family car. It is doubtful that any of the medical personnel who treated the little girl knew that this was a suicide attempt. On some level, however, her father understood. "He never touched me after the accident," she says now. "And do you know what is even stranger? In going through the family album, I discovered a small ballet program stuck in about halfway through the book. I was in that dance recital when I was 6. There are no more mementos of me—or of my three brothers—for the next seven years. That was the year my only sister was born. My father was very excited that we had another little girl in the family."

For over two decades, Connie "forgot" the molestation, the attempted drowning, and her decision to jump from the car. What she could not leave behind, however, was the deep sense of shame. The abuse by her father had been terrifying and painful. It was quite clear that she was not worth much if she was treated with such contempt. Her anguished feelings were overwhelming, but the pillow stuffed over her mouth formed both a command and a threat: "Don't tell!"

When she found the courage to tell anyway, her mother's reaction stunned her. "She acted as if I was an evil child; as if I made those awful things happen," Connie said. Rather than receiving comfort and protection, Connie was attacked and shamed again. Her mother's response as well as her father's abuse felt like attempted murders to the distraught child.

The message that her parents seemed to want her dead was powerful—so powerful it propelled her out of a moving vehicle. The suicide attempt was Connie's way of following through on her parents' "wishes." In the years that followed, burying the traumatic memories was another attempt at a type of death. As Dr. Bernie Siegel has pointed out, cutting off from our real feelings is an effective way to internalize the "die" message.[2] It is a rejection of the inner self, of our spiritual life. As long as Connie split off from her real feelings, the little girl inside her was obsessed with suicide, still trying to "kill" a very real part of herself.

Telling the Story of Abuse

In one sense, however, the "don't talk" rule helped Connie survive in a dysfunctional family. She learned all too soon that admitting your pain in a shame-based family stigmatizes you. Finding a setting where you can break this rule safely is the first thing victims must do on the road to recovery. Telling the story of child sexual abuse is a tremendously difficult step. It requires loving support from others who understand that sharing this secret feels like a mortal risk.

If a child who has been sexually abused has family members who can give a nonblaming, loving response to her disclosure, the impact of the trauma is greatly reduced. It is not, however, eliminated. Child sexual abuse inevitably causes damage, and recovery requires a respect for the tremendous losses involved. It is also important to realize that just because a child comes from a loving family, she will not necessarily tell a parent that she has been molested. Most children (especially after about age 3) instinctively understand that the molestation was an assault on their dignity and personhood—even if the abusive acts were not violent. The sense of shame can be overwhelming and the child's natural emotional response is to deny and suppress the reality of what has happened. This type of denial is a critical survival technique extremely useful for anyone facing danger. At these times, the unconscious shuts down our feelings, in effect "postponing" them until there is time, energy, and support to deal with the pain safely.

Once past that first stage of shock, however, a child may begin to reach out to others to help resolve those feelings. That is the moment when family rules will either allow her to move toward resolution or push her farther and farther into isolation, shame, and secrecy. Figure 2 deals with this dynamic, illustrating how *group process is critical to recovery from child sexual abuse.*

It is important to remember that no matter how faulty the response, the *act or acts of sexual abuse caused the initial damage to the survivor.* Whatever the parental shortcomings of Connie's mother, she was not responsible for her husband's incestuous attacks on her daughter. Connie's father made the decisions that resulted in the molestation and caused his daughter years of pain. Unfortunately, Connie's mother added a different type of damage through her abusive and shaming reaction to the disclosure. Since both parents were unwilling to talk about the incest, Connie's path toward recovery was blocked.

The response of those around the sexually abused child makes the difference in how free that child is to go through the recovery process. If the family denies the abuse and/or blames and shames the child (the process shown on the left side of the figure), she has little opportunity to recover. Her natural response is to split off from her real self and repress her memories in order to survive on a day-to-day basis within a dysfunctional system.[3]

It is important to emphasize, however, that someone who was blocked from recovery as a child does not have to be "stuck" there until her family recovers and can be

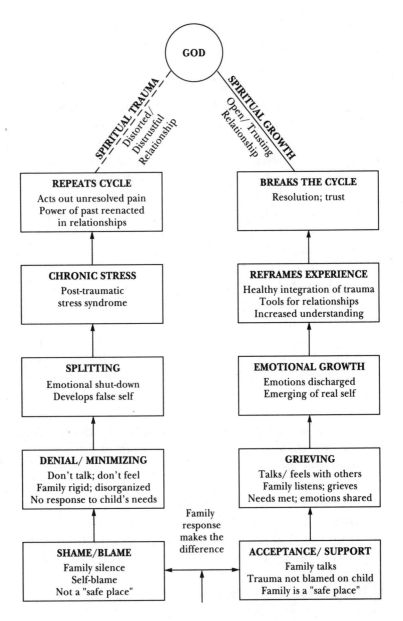

Figure 2. Response to Child Sexual Abuse

supportive. With families of origin like Connie's, this might never occur. The deep sense of shame that plagues survivors is a response to the stigma of child sexual abuse. Isolated by their shame, the survivors are cut off from community and others. Getting past that isolation and finding a healing community or "family" that can allow the truth to be told and feelings to be expressed (without stigmatizing, blaming, or "fixing") is the key to recovery from shame.

A New Family

During Connie's senior year in high school, she attended a youth meeting sponsored by a Christian group. The group leader talked about having a personal relationship with God, a concept Connie found exciting but out of reach. "I think it would be fantastic to have that, but I don't know how you get faith if you don't have it already," she told him. He took her interest seriously (a new experience for Connie), and they spent the next hour reviewing Bible verses. She was hungry for the message that she was precious to God and that Christ's death had freed her from the need to "earn" the love God had for her. With the leader's encouragement, she prayed and asked Christ to come into her life.

Connie's conversion experience introduced her to a new "family" of faith, which she embraced with enthusiasm. Her college years centered on Bible studies and Christian activities, and it seemed natural to move into a campus ministry position after graduation. The next years were, she says, the happiest in her life. Her supervisor, Larry, modeled and encouraged a strong sense of community. He talked to every one of the team members weekly and listened intently as they shared not only their experiences in ministry, but also their feelings. Larry gave Connie opportunities to lead and teach groups and encouraged her to believe in herself. Just as important, Larry and his wife June often invited Connie into their home, and she watched the mutual respect Larry and June gave each other and their child. "I watched them deal with their little girl and I would be shocked. They even disciplined her in a respectful way. I kept wondering, 'Aren't you going to shame her now?' but they didn't." While Connie had not yet recovered her memories of incest, she was in fact building the concept of a healthy family that would be critical to her eventual healing.

After several years in this encouraging environment, she decided to apply to seminary for formal training in ministry. Her personal crisis with incest memories came just a few months later. Her experience in campus ministry had convinced her that a nurturing community was vital, especially given the tremendous pain her therapy was uncovering, but she soon discovered that finding that at seminary or in the local church was not going to be easy.

"My therapist was a great support, but how was I going to live between sessions? My seminary classes were academic, not relational. I was learning a lot about Scripture and theology but there was very little emphasis on community or process. My fear and shame weren't relieved by theological concepts, no matter how sound. While I did find two professors very kind and helpful, they weren't able to give me the kind of support I needed to cope with the tremendous amount of inner pain I was feeling.

"About that time, I went to a Christian conference on overcoming depression and when it was over I was furious. The book table was covered with books on self-esteem and I wanted to throw them at somebody. I wanted to scream, 'I've bought the books and the tapes. I've listened to the lectures. It doesn't help; I am still depressed and I have absolutely no self-esteem! I don't need another book. I need *another person!*"

As her memories became more and more painful and shame-filled, Connie felt increasingly isolated from the Christian community she had assumed was there for her. Some friends reached out and listened. More, however, were horrified as she shared her incest memories, and responded with the same "don't talk" message her family had taught her. They were particularly distressed at how angry she was becoming, and how long the process of healing and forgiveness was taking. "I wanted to be airlifted out of the pain," Connie admitted, "and most of the Christians around me wanted this kind of 'rescue' for me too. They would suggest we 'just get down on our knees and give this to God.' When that didn't make the pain go away, they were annoyed with me."

When she poured out feelings of anger, shame, and self-hatred to one close Christian friend and church leader, he became visibly agitated. He suddenly interrupted her with, "But Connie, are you getting *better?*"

"That made me just shut down inside," she remembered, "because of course, I wasn't getting better at the time. The therapy, the returning memories, the dreams, were all increasing my awareness of inner pain. All the evidence indicated that it was getting worse.

"I realize now, however, that my friend had the

question wrong. If a woman was having cancer surgery and he ran into the operating theater and screamed, 'Are you getting *better?*' the answer would have to be 'No!' After all, they've just opened her up. She is bleeding, and her guts are all over the place! But the question isn't whether she is getting better; the question that should be asked is, 'Are you getting it *All?*' "

"If grief and pain are sometimes necessary for growth of the person, then we must learn not to protect people from them automatically as if they were always bad," Abraham Maslow noted. "Sometimes they may be good and desirable in view of the ultimate good consequences. Not allowing people to go through their pain and protecting them from it, may turn out to be a kind of overprotection, which in turn implies a certain lack of respect for the integrity and the intrinsic nature and the future development of the individual."[4]

Respectful treatment of people's very real distress is not only a prescription for psychological health, but also a very biblical concept for spiritual health.

The Bethany Model for Mourning

One of the most reassuring truths of Scripture is that Jesus didn't go around telling people who were grieving to cheer up, or denying their pain. In fact, he usually affirmed their mourning and grief, and often (as in the case of Lazarus's death) joined in their sorrow. Jesus was a man who was much criticized by religious leaders of his day because of his *joie de vivre.* He enjoyed nonkosher celebrations ("A law-breaker!" his critics shrilled), well-catered parties ("A wine bibber and glutton!" they reported), and fast company ("He dines with publicans and sinners!" they muttered). Obviously, he was not a long-faced or humorless man. Yet he blessed those who wept and mourned (Luke 6:21b). This *recognition and honoring* of the real feelings of others brings tremendous healing. The wisdom of the injunction in Romans 12:15 to "Rejoice with those who rejoice and weep with those who weep" is clear to anyone who has been part of a support group. It is this "mirroring" or reflecting back by others that gives the support group its great therapeutic powers, particularly when the issue is a deep sense of shame.

As long as the destructive "don't talk" message is obeyed, however, and the truth is repressed, *shame cannot be overcome*. It is helpful for survivors of incest (and survivors of all types of shame-based families) to look carefully at the scriptural model for handling shame. It is particularly helpful to review the method Jesus used to confront denial and to overcome the shame-based messages not only of society, but also of his own followers.

At the end of the Gospels, we find the "family" of disciples divided by a deep sense of shame over Jesus' message during the last weeks and months of his ministry. The "secret" that Jesus insisted on proclaiming was that he was going to be killed. The fact that this upset the disciples is certainly understandable. Many of these people had left families and livelihoods to follow this young rabbi. Most were convinced he was the promised Messiah and that God was going to use Jesus to deliver the people from Roman oppression. Until just weeks before his execution, Jesus' disciples were squabbling over who would sit on the right or left of his throne once he became King of Israel (Mark 10:35–45). Jesus' talk of imminent death not only dashed these expectations of powerful government careers, it also signaled the end of any hope for a political and spiritual revolution.

Shortly after a public appearance in which Jesus preached to over four thousand people and healed the lame, blind, and mute, the identity of this new prophet became a popular topic of conversation. Jesus asked his disciples who people thought he was.

They replied, "Some say John the Baptist; others say Elijah; and still others, Jeremiah or one of the prophets."

"But what about you?" he asked. "Who do you say I am?"

Simon Peter answered, "You are the Christ, the Son of the living God."

Jesus replied, "Blessed are you, Simon, son of Jonah, for this was not revealed to you by man, but by my Father in heaven." (Matt. 16:14–17)

At this moment, the faith of his followers was renewed and refreshed. Convinced they were on the verge of triumph and success, his disciples were confused when Jesus immediately began proclaiming not victory, but disaster.

From that time on Jesus began to explain to his disciples that he must go to Jerusalem and suffer many things at the hands of the elders, chief priests, and teachers of the law, and that he must be killed and on the third day be raised to life. (Matt. 16:21)

Just as Connie's Christian friends wanted God to "rescue" her from the situation, Jesus' disciples desperately resisted the idea that shame and death were ahead. Their response was to try to discourage Jesus from this defeatist talk and to deny the reality of what he was predicting. The disciple who had just proclaimed Jesus the Christ seems the most embarrassed and most anxious to deny this bizarre new message.

Peter took him aside and began to rebuke him. "Never Lord!" he said. "This shall never happen to you!" Jesus turned and said to Peter, "Get behind me, Satan! You are a stumbling block to me; you do not have in mind the things of God, but the things of men." (Matt. 16:22)

Jesus' resistance to the "don't talk" message continued in the days that followed. He continued not only to speak of his death, but also to specifically prophesy public mockery, flogging, and crucifixion at the hands of the very Romans the disciples had hoped to overthrow (Matt. 20:19). The stigma of such a death was anathema to his followers. Not only would it insure the defeat of their cause and the loss of their leader, but also their own religious laws held that someone who died in this manner was accused by God (Deut. 21:23). If Jesus died in this way, rather than being recognized as the Son of God, the stigma would forever isolate him from even the presence of God.

It is at this moment of deep division in the beginning Church that a story is told of one disciple who chose not to deny, but to accept and to mourn the death Jesus predicted. At a dinner party in her family home, Mary of Bethany anointed Christ's feet with an expensive perfume often used for embalming of the dead. Judas expressed anger at her extravagance (John 12:1–8); the money spent on the perfume could have been used for the poor! Jesus, however, allowed himself to be comforted by her love and her sorrow. He did not leap up and announce, "It's okay Mary, I'll *only* be dead three days!"

He did not minimize her pain or his own. He accepted her gift of mourning and reproved her critics:

> "Leave her alone," Jesus replied. "It was intended that she should save this perfume for the day of my burial. You will always have the poor among you, but you will not always have me." (John 12:7)

Two other gospel writers tell the story of the same grieving ritual taking place at the home of Simon the Leper (Matt. 26:6–13; Mark 14:3–9), although Mary is not named (some Bible scholars believe that these passages describe a similar ritual performed by a second woman in the same town; others believe they tell the same story and that Mary is again the woman described). When the disciples try to shame her, Jesus insists, "She has done a beautiful thing to me . . . when she poured this perfume on my body, she did it to prepare me for burial."[5]

Jesus had been predicting his death for months; yet in each story, the woman was apparently alone as she ritualized her grief for the terrible loss of the Messiah. Although the disciples argued that it was the waste of money that bothered them, in fact, it was the acknowledgment of impending death that offended and embarrassed them. Realizing their denial, Jesus emphasized the very message they resisted: "You will *not* always have me with you."

The woman's ritual may indicate that she was a professional mourner, a biblical career that has a long and respected history among Jewish women. Mourners were routinely called to weep and grieve for the dead in this culture. Not only were they skilled in preparing the body according to Jewish law, but also their wails and laments helped free the family and friends of the dead to express their sorrow and feel supported by the community in their grief. The people who watched the anointing of Jesus recognized that this was a death ritual. The grieving woman was, in fact, acting as if the body of Jesus was already dead; she was embalming a living "corpse." No wonder the disciples were alarmed and insulted!

Jesus, however, responded with gratitude and praise. He saw this ceremony as an act of faith and loving support for the most painful part of his ministry. Turning to the crowd in Simon's home, Jesus exclaimed, "Wherever this gospel is preached throughout the world, what she has done will also be told, in memory of her" (Mark 14:9).

It is significant that this example of grieving apparently had little impact on the disciples' denial. The same men who disapproved of this ritual continued to be nonplussed at Jesus' sermons. During the Last Supper, Jesus went through his own symbolic enactment of impending death by breaking bread ("This is my body, broken for you") and predicted his betrayal by all present. Their reaction was confusion and resistance.

Later, in the Garden of Gethsemane, Jesus grieved over the ordeal ahead. The pain he felt was so intense that he told the three disciples with him, "My soul is overwhelmed with sorrow to the point of death" (Mark 14:34). After asking them to "keep watch," he stepped forward to pray through his agony for deliverance. "Abba, Father," he said, "Everything is possible for you. Take this cup from me. Yet not what I will, but what you will" (Mark 14:36). The prayer was desparate. Luke records that "being in anguish, he prayed more earnestly, and his sweat was like drops of blood falling to the ground" (Luke 22:44).

When he returned—three times—to the company of Peter, John, and James, however, Jesus found them asleep. They were unable to mourn their own loss, or even fully to recognize it. Physically tired and emotionally exhausted, they withdrew into sleep. When the soldiers arrived to arrest their leader, the disciples abandoned him.

After a night of mockery and torture, Jesus was paraded through the streets, carrying his own cross. The mob jeered at his shameful fate, but along the road to Golgotha and at the foot of his cross, there were women (while Mary of Bethany is not mentioned, many other Marys are named) who publicly mourned his death. Three days later, some of these same women arrived at the tomb to continue their ministry of mourning and were the first witnesses of the Resurrection.

Surviving the Stigma

It is important to point out that despite the fact that Jesus consistently told the truth, he was generally not supported, not believed, and his emotional needs were not met by even some of his closest friends. Often, survivors of child sexual abuse assume that if they had only talked about the abuse sooner, or told their story better, they would have been helped. Thus, they take responsibility for their shame and isolation. In fact, however, a survivor can do everything "right" (that is, tell her story to someone who should be supportive) and still be met by denial, minimization, and finally even abandonment. The key is not to take responsibility for others' reactions, but to keep telling the truth until you find your own Mary of Bethany, or preferably, a whole troop of "mourners" to walk you through to recovery.

Connie's search for community was finally rewarded when she asked church staff members if they could suggest someone who could give her emotional support during her crisis. They recommended Midge Finley. "Midge was completing her graduate work in psychology," Connie recalled. "She wasn't an incest survivor, but she had come through some painful personal experiences. She was not afraid of letting me talk. She didn't try to 'fix' my problem—she just listened to me and cared about me. Within a few months, we had a group of women incest survivors who met at church with Midge and another group leader to tell our stories and to grieve.

"Recovery for me came through this process. It meant going through the pain, not getting away from it. My therapist walked with me through the memories, and Midge and my support group walked with me through the grief." While Connie did not receive an instantaneous healing, she did sense a spiritual renewal. "I experienced the presence of God even in the midst of this pain," she recalled. "Where was he? I feel he was in my therapist. I feel he has been in Midge and my friends in the group. That is where I've touched and experienced God. The members of the support group were survivors of a tremendous depth of pain themselves and they were able to hear and accept an incredible intensity of emotion. They could accept that these terrible things had happened and that my pain was important. They accepted my anger. They accepted my despair. I was suddenly free to express my real feelings. This kind of acceptance of the worst you have to offer, the most shameful things you feel, is so healing. Because they could accept me, I began to accept myself."

Connie's eloquent description shows how emotional growth follows grieving within an accepting "family" of supporters. No longer isolated in shame, the survivor's experience in the support group gives her new tools to review and reframe the trauma. "In the depth of my depression there were two things I could never get enough of," Connie recalled. "The first was encouragement that I would not always be in this pain and the second was that I was not alone. I received that from the support group."

Vehicles of Shame

Among these supporters, the stigma of being a victim was finally banished. This acceptance gave Connie the courage to explore the secrets of her past. Over the next year, her memories and her discussions with family members revealed clues to a multigenerational cycle of abuse. She discovered that her sister, Jean, had also been sexually molested by their father. Later, Jean was also involved in an incestuous relationship with one of her older brothers.

"As my memories came back over that year," Connie said, "I remembered fragments of things my father would say while he was molesting me. Usually, he was drunk and angry and talkative. On several of those terrible nights, he told me his mother had molested *him*."

As Connie pieced together memories, looked at pictures, and talked to her therapist, it became clear that her father was not just a "heavy drinker," he was an alcoholic. Two of her brothers, moreover, were already in the early stages of alcohol addiction.

"It still seems incredibly unfair, all that family pain. I look at the wasted lives and the suffering and it is hard to come to terms with it. The early deaths of my grandfather and father, the alcoholism of my father and my brothers, the sexual abuse that linked my grandmother, my father, my sister, my brother, and me in multigenerational anguish. There was such isolation, such shame."

Determined to escape that isolation, Connie continued to share the truth of her family story in therapy and in group. As she talked about the old secrets, a new understanding and acceptance of self emerged. Three years after her work with incest memories began, she explained, "I am just beginning to see the patterns, to understand the forces involved. For example, cars have been an unconscious symbol of my family's shame and self-destruction. I've discovered that three generations of family members have used cars to express 'die' messages. I've also learned that in dream imagery, a car is often a symbol for the ego.

"My dad's father committed suicide but no one ever talked about it. My mother said my father told her two different stories about the suicide. One was that Grandpa shot himself, another that he poisoned himself. After checking with relatives, I found out that my grandfather had committed suicide in his car. He had shut the windows and doors to the garage and run the car's motor. So the cause of death was monoxide poisoning, which explains one of Dad's stories.

"Just a few days before the suicide, however, my dad—who was 15 at the time—had taken the car without my grandfather's permission. My grandfather had punished him severely when he returned. My therapist suggested that in his mind, my dad may have felt he put the 'gun'—in this case a car—to his father's head.

"I did not consciously know this 'secret' story when I jumped out of the car; but I chose the most powerful image available to get through to my father. My father's own death when I was a teenager also involved a car. He had been drinking and driving on Christmas Eve and he had an accident on a deserted country road. The accident was minor, and if he had been sober, he probably would have survived. He died of exposure, next to the car.

"Fifteen years later, I burned out my car's motor and went into a suicidal depression. I still have to watch myself carefully when I drive. It is an easy and dangerous place to follow through on self- destructive messages. I respect the power of those unconscious symbols, but I can face my family's pain—pain that has been hidden for generations. I don't have to be de- stroyed by shame any longer.

"From the outside looking in, however, none of that pain was obvious. The fact that my family was so functional made it easy to deny the problems, to avoid seeing the patterns. My dad was well known in his field and he made a substantial fortune. My family built a dream home in the country and when I was 10, my parents gave me a horse. To the people who knew us, we looked like a very successful, very normal family," Connie said. Then she smiled. "But we did have a lot of car trouble."

Chapter 3

THE SURVIVOR AND FAMILY

Donna was intent on wrapping a Christmas gift with ribbon that refused to lie flat, when she heard her mother's voice: "Julie, honey, why don't you and Grandpa go down the hill and get some holly for the mantle?" She felt her mouth go dry as she watched her 5-year-old daughter disappear out the door. Donna's father followed Julie without a backward glance.

Her sister was sitting on the couch playing with her baby. Her brother-in-law was stretched out on the floor with the sports section. Her cousin was on the phone with her grandmother.

"It was all so normal, so pretty," Donna said. "Like a modern Currier and Ives print. I wanted to scream, 'Julie can't be alone with him!' But I couldn't. It all happened so fast. They were outside. It all looked so harmless. . . .

"If I yelled, everyone would think I was crazy. So I said nothing and I *felt* crazy.

"As I thought about it, I realized that my mother often set up situations where kids are alone with my father. I've told her he can't be alone with Julie. I have told her he molested us as kids. But if I'd said, 'Julie can't go with him!' she'd have said, 'Oh don't be silly,

Donna. It's just down the road' and everyone would have supported her. I'd have looked like a fool.

"On the other hand, when I didn't say anything, my mother gave me this little satisfied glance as if to say, 'You see? Even you think he is really safe! Nothing ever really happened!'

"You have to understand that my mother acts like a mother on a television sitcom in the fifties. You know, the ones with lines like, 'Want another cookie, dear?' She is petite, fine-boned, and looks like she was born wearing pearls and beige linen. Her hair is a beautiful shade of gray. She still goes to the women's missionary society at church.

"But this is also the woman who slept through my childhood. When my sister and I left for school and when we came home, we had to be careful not to wake her up. She always seemed to be floating—just out of reach. She didn't work outside the home. She just wasn't there emotionally at all.

"My father was the dominant force at home—and everywhere else. He would yell and put her down and she would just act long-suffering. But outside the home, he was charming. Pushy, maybe, but charming. He was the principal of the local Christian high school, head of the board of deacons, and he and mother were the youth group sponsors."

The "Perfect" Family

"I had the perfect family. Everyone said so. I can't remember a time when people didn't tell me how lucky I was to have my parents," Donna said. "I always said, yes, I certainly was. Then one day, a woman at church was gushing on about my parents and she said, 'You must have had a *wonderful* childhood.'

"Something just snapped inside. I said, 'No, I had a terrible childhood.'

"She looked at me as if I had lost my mind. Then she said firmly, 'No you didn't,' and walked away!"

People have tremendous resistance to hearing a child's pain. The desire to discount and deny it is overwhelming. This is true even in cases where physical abuse has left repeated bruises. In sexual abuse, where there may be no physical evidence at all, the denial is far easier.

Roland Summit points out that people who had untroubled childhoods resist identification with issues of victimization. Believing that it can happen requires changing their views about happy childhoods and a just and fair society. It is easier to believe that the child is misled, confused, or even malicious. On the other hand, the many adults who were sexually assaulted as children are often extremely reactive against the whole issue. If they have repressed their memory, they "feel unexplainable pain and anger with any reminder."[1]

Within the family, there are strong motivations to deny and cover up the truth. A study by Diana E. H. Russell documents that the more closely related the child is to the perpetrator, the less likely she is to be supported by anyone she tells.[2] The child who is being sexually abused—especially if the abuser is a family member—is encouraged to act as if everything were normal. Yet everything within her says that this is not normal or fine or okay. If she struggles to tell the truth about what is going on, she often discovers that the response is clear: You are crazy, you are making it up.

You asked for it or you exaggerated it. You are the problem. Nothing—or nothing important—ever happened.

A child will be even more uncertain about what she believes or experiences if a domineering parent is the family's only "authority" about what is true. Donna said, "Once when Julie was at my parents house, my father insisted she had three ears. His teasing was relentless. It was the same attitude he had with me all those years, 'What I say is true and what you say isn't.' Once I saw him shove my 6-year-old nephew and then laugh and deny it.

"It isn't that we all really believe my father. But after a while, we don't believe ourselves."

This is how the betrayal of a child's sense of herself begins. She will simply begin to act as if everything is fine and disregard the pain within. Eventually, however, the pain in Donna's past began to turn up in recurring depression. Her marriage was rapidly breaking up. Entering therapy for relief, she assumed that she was the only problem. She spent hours telling the therapist how "wonderful" her parents had been, and then would share her memories of her distant, "Sleeping Beauty" mother and her authoritarian and seductive father.

As she talked about her childhood, it became clear that Donna's family was far from perfect. "I remember lying in my bed at night and seeing my dad come in and sit on my sister's bed," she told the therapist. "Jan was in junior high then and just developing breasts. He used to rub them and talk to her. I remember that she and I sat in the closet together one day and she told me how much she wished Dad would stop that. 'It really hurts my boobs!' she told me.

"We never had privacy. Dad was always watching us. He used to put his hands on us when no one was watching, then deny it. I remember that he once checked Jan under her pants to 'see if she had hair yet.'"

At this point, Donna's therapist was convinced that Donna was a survivor of sexual abuse. Even though Donna's own memories were limited to a conviction that "something" had happened to her when she was 4, the therapist felt that her memory blocks were typical of incest survivors. It should be added that even if Donna's victimization had been limited to watching her sister being molested, it is significant and would have had a tremendous impact. A seductive parent can harm an entire family system even if only one, or even none, of the children are physically molested. Moreover, the molestation does not have to involve penetration to be harmful.

At her therapist's suggestion, Donna joined a church-based support group for survivors. The group gave Donna new perspective on how many different types of families hide the secret of child sexual abuse. Some of the women—like Connie—also had had "picture-perfect" families with hidden issues. It was during a group session that the memory that "something terrible" had happened when she was 4 became more specific.

"I told the group that I remembered being in a bathroom with gymnasium green tiles. To this day I won't wear anything green! I told them I remembered my dad telling me to get in the shower and feeling like I didn't want to do it. I pointed to his penis and asked, 'What's that, Daddy?' That is where my memory had always stopped.

"And then, as I was talking to the group, everything

that happened next came back. I could feel Daddy lifting me up while the water sprayed us both. He held me against his erect penis. 'It's a horsey,' he said. There was a sharp pain in my butt and I was being jolted up and down. I remember my ponytail bouncing on my back while my feet dangled high above the shower floor. There was an explosion inside me and sticky liquid was all over my bottom. Daddy washed me off and I cried, 'I didn't mean to, Daddy, it just exploded!'

"The full feeling inside my rectum made me run to the toilet. I started to scream, 'I gotta go poop and I can't!' I sat on the toilet, shivering. Then I ran, ran to my room and hid in the closet. I can still feel jagged edges of the textured wall poking my naked back while I cried. I knew what had happened was terrible and that it was my fault.

"Then I heard him in the next room saying, 'Aren't you dressed yet, Donna? Get out here right now.' My dripping bottom felt torn and raw. I stood up, fists and teeth clenched tight and I whispered, 'I hate you. I hate you forever.'"

"'The group was silent for a long time. Then the leader said, 'There is a word for what happened to you. Do you know what it is?' I shook my head. She told me, 'That is called sodomy.'"

"Am I Making All This Up?"

When survivors dare to examine their memories as Donna did, family members will most often resist and sabotage their efforts. One woman had been molested by her father when she was 2. After the molestation, he took out a gun and shot her and himself. He died immediately but the bullet only grazed her temple. When she was 15, she asked her mother about the scar. "You fell down," her mother told her.

For Donna, the scars were internal and even easier for her family to deny. Without giving them any details, Donna told her family that her father had molested her as a child and that she also remembered that he had molested her sister. She announced that her daughter, Julie, would no longer be allowed to be alone with her father.

Her father categorically denied everything. Her sister said she was exaggerating and her mother became agitated at Donna's "ruining a good man's reputation." She reminded Donna that she was "artistic" and "creative" and "imaginative." She also did everything she could to sabotage Donna's rule that Julie could not be alone with her grandfather.

By the next time she met with the group, Donna was beside herself with anxiety. "I think I made everything up! I must have ! Sometimes I can't remember anything. Sometimes I remember only in flashes. It took me three months to remember how old I was when I got my ears pierced! There is something terribly wrong with my ability to remember—how can I trust it?"

"Memory gaps are typical for people who had traumatic childhoods," the group leader observed. "It seems unlikely to me that you would make up the story of your experience in the shower. For one thing, it wasn't what you expected to remember, was it?"

"No," Donna said, "I knew that whatever happened to me at 4 was scary and I didn't want to think about it, but I suppose my greatest fear was that it was intercourse."

"And instead," the group leader said slowly, "it was a

type of abuse for which you didn't even have a grown-up word, right?"

Donna nodded, but the miserable fear that she had "made up" her memories would haunt her for months. In individual meetings with her own therapist, he pointed out to her that she didn't have much motive for making up a memory that obviously gave her deep pain. He also noted that her physical sensations and words were the ones a young child would have. "The pain and the specific physical reactions don't sound like fantasies, Donna. They sound like a remarkably accurate description," he told her.

Still, Donna resisted accepting the memory as the truth. At the group's suggestion, however, she began to verify specific aspects of what she had remembered. She still did not tell her mother about the shower incident, but she began to check out the details. She asked her mother if there was anything different about the walls of the house they had lived in at the time of the attack. Her mother recalled that they were "textured and rough—just covered with sharp little points!" In subsequent conversations, she also confirmed that the bathroom tiles were green, and that she often put Donna's hair up in a shoulder-length ponytail when she was 4.

That week in group, Donna said, "Mom also told me that when I was four, I once came running into her room late at night. I had awakened after a nightmare. 'Help!' I cried, 'I'm afraid I'll turn into a mother.' I'm sure I had only a vague idea of how sex and having babies were connected; I wonder, did that attack in the shower cause my terror? All of those years that I didn't remember the abuse consciously—my junior high and high school years—I told everyone that I didn't want to be a mother.

"Oh—and Mom remembered that I was worried that year about 'Bombs exploding,'" Donna added. "It didn't hit me until I mentioned it just now that that is the word I used in the shower, 'It just *exploded*, Daddy.'"

Rediscovering the Family Story

At this point, Donna decided to scratch the surface of her "perfect family" a little further. The next week, she told the group, "During my junior year, a girl from church lived with us while her parents were going through a divorce. I called Cheryl to ask if Dad had ever come on to her when she stayed with us. She said Dad had put his hands under her blouse and kissed her on the lips several times but she said she was 'so hungry for affection' that she never protested.

"I talked with Aunt Susan, my mother's sister, last night and told her what I was going through. She just sighed and said, 'Oh, honey.' Then she told me that Dad had started trying to kiss and touch her when she was still a teenager and he had just married her sister. She talked to Mom several times about it and Mom always said she'd talk to Dad.

"When I asked her why she never turned him in, she said, 'I thought it was all my fault and I never thought he'd touch you kids.' She also said she did it to protect Mom, that she didn't want to hurt her."

Later, Donna discovered two other young women who had been victimized by her father. Both were graduates of the high school where he was a principal and neither of them would testify against him. "I'll deny it if you say anything," one told her.

Concerned about the number of other girls who had been victimized by her father, Donna bought several books on "good" and "bad" touching to review with her daughter Julie. Julie listened quietly and then told her that yes, that had happened to her. "Was it Grandpa?" Donna asked. "No, it was Daddy. He tried to get me to touch him down there too, but I always ran away."

Donna had been divorced from Ben for a year and it had been six months since Julie had been with her father. "Half the time I think I should have known. The other half I think I somehow talked her into believing she was molested. I am sure that is what Ben would say!"

"Last Tuesday, after my conversation with Julie," Donna continued, "I prayed for help with my depression. I poured out my fears that I was hurting my father, that my memories were misleading me and maybe Julie. Suddenly, I got this strong sense that I should visit Grandma, my father's mother. It was a hassle—Julie had a cold and didn't want to go. It was a forty-five-minute drive one way. Still, I gave Grandma a call and she said, 'Oh Donna, I'd love to see you and Julie.'

"When I got there, we sat down and chatted on her couch while Julie watched television. I noticed her old scrapbooks on the wall and took down the oldest one. The first picture was a portrait of her at a dance. It was in the 1930s and she was standing in front of a potted plant. Her hair was swept up with a feather pinned across the back. Her face looked young, wide-eyed. Her dress looked like silk.

"Oh that dress!' Grandma told me. 'That dress was sinfully expensive. My father paid twenty-five dollars for it! Absolutely unheard of in our family!' We looked at the other pictures in the album, but Grandma kept returning to the subject of the dress she wore to the dance. 'So expensive!' she remembered, shaking her head.

"Suddenly, she became agitated. 'I really shouldn't tell you this,' she said. I said, 'Grandma, you don't have to tell me anything you don't want to.'

"I really shouldn't tell you this. But he raped me.'

"Who raped you?'

"George—your grandfather.'

"When?'

"After the dance, of course,' she said, thumbing the album. 'It was our first date. We drove home together and he pulled off the road. He pushed me, and . . . he . . . he just raped me. I didn't know what he was doing. He tore my dress. When he finished, he just said, 'You haven't done this before, have you?'"

"I was crying. I said, 'No.'"

"He told me that he had done it once before. He said he had to because the girl had pushed up against him. I went home and got up the stairs somehow. The dress was ruined. I bled—on my, how I bled. But I never told anyone.'"

When Donna finished telling the group the story, she added, "My grandmother married George later that same year. He died last February. She kept the rape a secret for fifty-three years."

Giving Up the Idealized Family

After the visit with her grandmother, Donna found a new determination not to hang on to family secrets any longer. Since her mother and father refused to listen to the truth, she decided not to spend her summer holidays with them at the beach, and explained why. Her mother became very upset and sent her a gift book about forgiving "misunderstandings."

Her sister called and told her in an accusing voice that she was "killing Dad" and that he was "terribly depressed over all of this." Everyone implied that Donna was taking out the unhappiness of her divorce on her family.

"They keep saying I should forgive and forget," she told the group. "But they won't admit there is really anything to forgive! I wrote my mother a letter and quoted from Lewis Smedes's book *Forgive and Forget* in explaining that the truth has to be faced before reconciliation can work.[3] She was furious! She wants me just to drop everything. She wants a kind of forgiveness that is just forgetfulness. It makes me crazy. I just can't go home right now if that is the price tag. I hope," she added softly, "that God understands that. My mother implies that if I were really a Christian, I would come home."

"It sounds like home doesn't feel very safe to you right now," the support leader observed.

"I don't believe that God wants people to enter burning houses, Donna, do you?" Connie asked.

Donna's head went up. "You know, that's exactly what it's like! I need to get out of a burning house. I need to get some fresh air and find a safe place. Later, maybe I can go inside and fix things up a little, but first we need to get some water on that house!"

Connie nodded. "Also, Donna, you need to first figure out that the house *is* burning down. If you go outside for a while you can see that. You need some distance to figure out that this is really an unhealthy family."

Donna laughed. "Yes, otherwise I think, 'Gee, I can't see and my eyes are streaming; I must have vision problems!'"

"Try thinking, 'It's smoke! The house is on *Fire!*'" Connie said.

"Help! I can't breathe!" Donna cried.

By this time, the whole group was giggling. "Asthma!" they called out. "You have emphysema!"

"I do think it's me most of the time," Donna admitted. "How can I really believe our house is 'on fire' when nothing is obviously wrong? My family still looks 'perfect' or at least 'nice' on the outside. Nobody gets drunk. Everyone is polite. What kind of a daughter would avoid such nice people?" she asks, shrugging.

For many survivors, Donna's ambivalence about detaching from her family even in small ways ("No, I can't spend the summer holidays with you this year") will be familiar. When a child has been abused the parental bond can retain a traumatic grip on the soul, keeping the child from moving into emotional and spiritual adulthood. To become an adult, the child needs a sense of self-worth and independent identity, tools the dysfunctional family cannot provide.

For the survivor of a dysfunctional home, the support group can provide a radically new model of family that supports recovery. Loving attention is given, yet this type of family love allows the child a sense of self based on the truth. In the safety of the group, the survivor can question or reexamine her dysfunctional family "rules" and "myths" without risking rejection. A new world of choices and independent action is modeled.

The typical survivor of a dysfunctional family was encouraged to take care of her parents, not herself. The payoff for worrying about her parents' needs and feelings was the hope that her parents would then turn around and take care of her needs and feelings. In fact, however, payday seldom, if ever, arrived.

This is the game most adult survivors still play with their families. The Inner Child clings to the hope that if she tries hard enough and denies her own needs and feelings long enough, her parents will reward her by taking care of those needs and feelings. This is a false and dangerous hope. It keeps victims locked in a no-win system. The strength of the system, however, is what leads to the desperate idealization of a troubled family. It is why Donna denied everything she really felt to protest that her family was "perfect." Healthy families don't need to be perfect—they can be real.

The realistic hope for survivors is that they can now do for themselves what their parents could not do. This is the first step toward spiritual and emotional health. Lying and pretending that nothing is wrong is not the way to "honor" parents. Taking care of oneself does not show disrespect toward one's family or others. In fact, it is the first step toward knowing how to really love. Christ's well-known command that we love others "as ourselves" requires developing some skill at healthy self-love.

Giving up idealized fantasy parents, however, can be extremely painful. It was this dream, after all, that got many survivors through the most painful parts of their past. Patience with this difficult process is essential. Trying to rush into adult development will not work. A survivor can approach the task of detaching and become a separate and more healthy adult in a variety of ways. *Not everyone needs to confront her perpetrator and her family as early in the process as Donna.* In some cases, of course, the perpetrator is dead or has lost contact with the survivor. In other cases, the family is literally the only support system a survivor has. For people in this situation, the first task is building new networks that will encourage health and growth. No one should ever be pushed into a confrontaton before they are ready. Even for those who choose to separate from toxic parents, the process can be gradual.

"Look, Donna," Connie said, "I took a year "off" from my family while I was working through my memories. Now I see them but I am very careful to schedule my time with them and limit it to short periods. Three hours is the maximum I can handle and I don't have to deal with the one who molested me—he died years ago. I do, however, have to deal with the people who did not protect me and did not believe me, so I make sure I have an appointment or have a friend pick me up by a certain deadline. And most important, I spend more time with the people who can support and encourage me and help me act in a healthy way. If I stay with my own family too long I start to think and act in the same old destructive ways."

The Victimization Cycle

"The thing I keep wondering," Donna said quietly, "is if there is some kind of crazy genetic pattern in all of this? After my divorce, I started dating a man who seemed so different from Ben. He was older and I trusted him. On our third date, he raped me. I said no. I screamed 'No!' He still raped me. Now, I discover that this is what happened on my grandparents' first date! As in my grandmother's case this was a man I might have married. Like my mother, I did marry a man who molested my daughter.

"When does it stop? How do I make sure that Julie doesn't carry on all of the unfinished sexual business of this family? And there is one more thing." Donna's voice dropped and became strained, "I'm scared to death that somehow, someday I'll abuse a child."

"When I hear about victims becoming victimizers, I panic. I was afraid to have a child; I don't babysit, and I'm scared to teach Sunday School. It's like having a brand on my soul; I feel like the 'bad seed.'"

The truth about the impact of victimization is far more complex and less frightening than the myth Donna absorbed. *Sexual acting out is a common symptom among molested children, but the majority of sexual abuse victims do not become adult perpetrators of child sexual abuse.* They may, in fact, become vigilant protectors of children—committed to keeping youngsters safe from sexual predators. On the other hand, some links with early experience and perpetration have been established: one study of males incarcerated for sex offenses found that 31 percent had been molested as children or teenagers.[4]

A few young victims become perpetrators almost immediately. The first study of children (ages 4–13) who molest other children found that 100 percent of the girls who had sexually abused younger children (including acts such as forcible penetration with a foreign object) had been molested themselves.[5] Only 49 percent of the boys who were identified as perpetrators, however, reported that they had been molested by an older child or adult.[6]

While the research makes it clear that there is nothing automatic about victims becoming perpetrators, it certainly indicates that victims are more at risk than nonvictims for a whole range of destructive sexual behaviors. Studies consistently find that a majority of prostitutes, for example, were molested as children. For this reason, it is critical for survivors to face the issue of sexuality honestly and to create new boundaries and new compassion for this traumatized area of the self.

Chapter 4

THE SURVIVOR AND SEXUALITY

"I was probably 2 or 3 years old the first time my father took me to a brothel," Gerri said. "I know I was no older than that, because I remember that I had curls and by the time I was 4, my hair was straight. There were several men lined up to have sex with me that night and I remember passing out with pain a couple of times. Once when I came to and opened my eyes, I saw my dad in the corner of the room with a prostitute leaning against him. She had on heavy makeup and a frilly dress. I remember thinking, 'I will *never* look like that.'"

"All of my life—even during the years I blocked out my memories—I have chosen neuter or masculine clothes," she said, "and I react badly to women dressed in fancy, ultrafeminine clothing. My youngest daughter, however, loves to wear ruffles and dresses. Actually, I enjoy letting her dress up and just in the last year, I have been able to choose some more feminine clothes. Not," motioning to her flannel shirt and jeans and laughing, "that you could tell it from this outfit."

Gerri paused to chew an almost nonexistent nail before she continued, "I don't know how often my dad brought me back but my last memory of the place was when I was about 8 years old. I have a lot of memories of cameras and pictures being taken. I've learned since then that the city we lived in at the time is a major center for child pornography and I assume my father was involved in that. I know that when I was 9, we moved to a different state and the sexual abuse stopped. We bought a house despite the fact that with my dad's employment record there was no way we should have been able to afford it. I wonder now if prostituting me was his way of getting the down payment."

The "Gift" of Shock

"Until about a year and a half ago, I had no conscious memories of the brothel or of anything else before we moved to the new house. The hardest thing for people to understand is why I didn't remember all of this for so long. My parents have written me several angry letters threatening to sue me for slander and one of my closest friends just doesn't believe that if all this really happened, I could have forgotten it.

"Several months ago I told my children that we couldn't go to visit their grandparents because they hurt me a long time ago and now they were lying and saying that I made it all up. My daughter said, 'Mommy, I am mad at Gram and Grandpop for hurting you, but I still love them.' I told her that it was okay for her to love them, but we just couldn't go to visit them because it was very hard on me. She understood that.

"I didn't go into any details about what had happened because my girls are so young. I just explained the return of my memories by telling them that when all of these bad things happened, God knew I could not think about them yet. It would have been too hard on me. So he allowed me to forget until I was ready to remember. I told them that there is something called shock that God gives us to protect us when something happens that is so awful our hearts cannot stand it. Shock makes us forget for a while so that our hearts won't break and we won't die."

As Gerri explained to her daughters, it is not unusual for the victims of traumatic events to experience a delay of months or even years before they have a conscious reaction or even a recollection of the trauma. Clinicians call this phenomenon Delayed Post-traumatic Stress Disorder. This delayed reaction is common (although not universal) among child sexual abuse survivors, and three of the other members of the group—Kate, Connie, and Donna—reported a similar delay in their memory of and their response to sexual abuse. Eventually, however, all four group members had "painful, intrusive recollections of the event or recurrent dreams or nightmares during which the event (was) reexperienced (DSM-III-R).[1]

Betrayal by Both Sexes

For Gerri, the memories returned during a visit with Helen, her neighbor. Helen was about a dozen years older than Gerri and had several teenage children. Over a period of several months, the women developed a close friendship. One afternoon, Gerri was sitting at the kitchen table chatting when she found herself staring at Helen's bare arm. It was fair and heavily freckled, just like the skin on her own mother's arms. Suddenly, scenes slipped into Gerri's consciousness, scenes that shook her to her depths.

"I remembered my father bringing me home and proudly telling my mother, 'She was the best little monkey in the whorehouse,'" Gerri said. "I remember that I showed her what I had learned and she slapped me. Later, however, she started doing sexual things with me."

"One of my issues with gender identity is that I was betrayed by both my mother and my father," confessed Gerri. "I am confused about *both* sexes! I think what I feel the most, however, is my lack of mothering. I think that is the quality I was especially attracted to in Helen."

The confusion could not have been introduced at a more delicate stage developmentally. "Existing evidence indicates that perhaps as early as age one but no later than age three, children come to think of themselves not as persons but as males or females, and that from then on gender identity is *the* cornerstone of the self-concept."[2] For Gerri, that cornerstone—one of the primary elements of the self (see figure 1, in chapter 1)—was badly fractured.

The experience also left her with a traumatized reaction to male genitals. "I've always thanked God I had daughters and not sons. I couldn't have dealt with little boys. I've babysat a few times and realized that just diapering them was difficult for me."

Only a toddler when she was gang-raped, Gerri had experienced searing physical pain that came back with the memory. "When I think about how small my vagina must have been. . . ." she said, shaking her head. "I do have several memories of prostituting that involve women clients. That surprises me, I guess. What I remember feeling when a woman came into the room was relief. I knew there wouldn't be any pain."

Despite her painful memories of heterosexual rape, Gerri noted, "I've always been straight and I really want my marriage to work on a sexual as well as an emotional level. Still, I have had a long struggle with my feelings about being a woman. Actually, my friendship with Helen has been enormously helpful with those feelings. I think she 're-parented' me in some ways.

My sister—who went through some of the same kind of abuse—has also had a lot of confusion and conflict around being female, but her reactions to men are even more negative than mine and she identifies herself as a lesbian."

While Gerri felt that her sister's rejection of heterosexual relationships was a result of the abuse—and some clinicians have speculated that traumatic sexualization might have this effect—research has so far failed to establish any evidence that lesbian behavior is more typical of the survivors of child sexual abuse.[3] Moreover, it is especially difficult to generalize about the impact on Gerri and her sister, since their abuse involved multiple female perpetrators, a situation that is rare and virtually unstudied.

While reports of females molesting children of either sex are increasing, they still represent only a small percentage of alleged cases. There is reason, however, to believe that these cases are underreported. The findings on the girls in the study of children who molest other children provide some clues to a sociological blindness on this issue. Although they comprise a smaller group, the girls who molested other children showed more sexual violence than the boys. Some of this group's victims (including both boys and girls) required medical attention; yet not one of the molesting girls was dealt with by the juvenile court system. Most of the boys were.[4] It may be that the view that only males molest others is so entrenched that even girls whose perpetrator behavior is extreme are not taken seriously.

There is no reason, however, to assume that being sexually abused by a female is less damaging than being abused by a male. Nicholas Groth has gathered sobering evidence connecting child sexual abuse with convictions for sex offenses. He notes that thirty-one percent of convicted male sex offenders report that they were the victims of child sexual abuse, and that forty-one percent of that group indicate they were molested as children by females.[5]

Incest Memories and Sexual Response

Gerri's sexual experiences with female and male perpetrators—and her life as a child prostitute—ended abruptly with the family's move out of state. "I'll never know what happened," Gerri said. "Whether my mother put her foot down and said, 'No more,' or whether just the change in neighborhoods made the difference. Maybe it had become dangerous. Maybe I was too old. I don't know.

"Suddenly I had to pretend to be a normal fourth grader. I guess it figures that I just blacked out everything I had seen. My adolescent years were stormy. Both of my parents hit me a lot when I was in junior high and high school, but the sexual touching stopped.

"I dated a lot in college but I didn't meet Bob until my senior year. We fell in love and started sleeping together. I thought sex was great. Then we got married and wham, sex was *not* great."

For the incest survivor, being married and becoming a family is fraught with dangerous connections. "Let's play house; you be the daddy and I'll be the mommy," children say. But when an adult couple "play house" and a man becomes "the daddy," it is a potent symbol of danger to the victim of child abuse. For Gerri, of course, both parental roles had been traumatically sexualized.

A couple years after their marriage, Gerri and Bob became Christians. "The church was a scary place for me," she remembered. "I didn't remember my childhood but I was afraid I wouldn't measure up somehow. Still, I took comfort in the doctrine of grace, in the whole idea that God had wiped away my guilt. I started to compulsively memorize Scripture. Those Scriptures turned out to be really valuable and comforting when my memories came back.

"At the time, though, I was just trying to be a nice Christian housewife. I became a mother. I led Bible studies. The church community was the center of my life for the next nine years. My marriage, however, was in trouble although we still slept together. Then I met Helen and my memories came back. All sex with Bob stopped soon after that. In fact all *conversation* stopped. This has been going on now for over fifteen months, but in the last couple of weeks, Bob—who refused to go to any counseling before—has started seeing a therapist. I don't know if the marriage is going to work, but it's a start."

Gerri added that not only was she no longer orgasmic, she actually had no feeling at all in her genital area.

"The loss of feeling started when the memories came back," she said. "I am on medication so that I can urinate. I just don't feel anything below the waist." Gerri had internalized the message of traumatic sexualization—"Don't feel!" (see figure 1)—in the most literal way imaginable.

"Every incest survivor I have ever met had sexual difficulties," Dr. Karin Meiselman has noted. "What is amazing, however, is the *range* of difficulties. I never cease to be amazed at the ingenuity of the human mind in developing coping systems."[6]

While Gerri's shutdown of all genital feeling is unusual, many survivors report that the "don't feel" message has a dramatic impact on their relationships. Connie noted, "For me, the response has been emotional as well as sexual—I'm just terrified of having a relationship. On the one hand, I have always wanted to date and marry. On the other, I know I send out 'go away' messages to any male I meet."

For many survivors, the fears about relationships and the loss of sexual desire begin or intensify when traumatic incest memories surface. "When I first got my memories back," Kate said, "I stopped dating. Instead, I went out with a group from work that included mostly gay men. I guess these were the only relationships that felt safe."

"I've had several periods in our marriage where making love literally made me nauseous," Ruth told the group. "I think one of the reasons John is paying for my therapy is this hope that it will 'fix' my sexual response. So far, I've spent the sessions talking about incest and I come home less interested in having sex than ever.

"Two weeks ago, John went in to see my therapist. He

told her that he couldn't take it anymore. 'I touch my wife and she looks like she's going to lose her lunch. I want a normal marriage; what can I do?' My therapist talked to him and I think he finally got the message that I wasn't just doing this to be difficult. It was the first time he had really sat down and listened to what had happened between me and Uncle Fred. I'd had a nightmare about Fred once and had kicked John out of bed! After he heard my story, that made sense to him."

In incest, the wrong people pay. Most often it is not the perpetrator but the friends, children, or spouse who feel the impact of the survivor's traumatic sexualization. Perspective for the people close to a survivor, particularly in the initial period of recovery, is a critical ingredient. Knowing that the loss of desire came from a memory he had nothing to do with eased John's pain, although he admitted to Ruth that he found it hard not to interpret her response as a rejection. Later, he joined a husband's support group, as did the husbands of Gerri, Alice, and Sharon. A male therapist volunteered to be the group leader and the four men met with him several times. The group helped John to see that he was not alone in his feelings of confusion and anger. Ruth noticed that his attitude toward her became much less defensive.

Sex: The Price of Affection?

"Last night, I tried to explain to John that I need affection, but pressuring me at all about sex right now feels familiar and painful," Ruth said. "Growing up, I honestly never felt valued for much of anything except for the sexual pleasure I gave to my uncle and later, to boyfriends.

"My father was always enraged with me, mainly because I upset my mother. My mother used my dad as a constant threat to keep the three of us children in line: 'Wait until I tell your father about this!' Since I was the oldest, and the most rebellious, I was usually the one who got belted.

"So, on the one hand, there was this very strict upbringing, but there were no protective boundaries for me at all. The protection was for Mom and Dad. I wasn't quite 12 years old when Uncle Fred started following me around. He and Aunt Marie had moved in with us just a few months earlier.

"At first, I liked the attention from a man. After all, the kind of attention I got from Dad was the end of the belt. It didn't take long, however, for me to get upset and tell my mother. My mother just told me to tell her sister, my aunt, and my aunt informed me that it was my fault and I should stay away from him.

"Since Fred and Marie lived upstairs, staying away from him was impossible. Everywhere I turned, he was there, like a fly on meat! I had given up getting any help from the other adults, so I just went along with him.

"One day, he took me over to his brothers' house and introduced me to them. He treated me like I was his private dirty joke. He hung on me and snickered, and from the way he acted, I realized that he wanted me to let them do the same things he was doing to me. There were no women in the house at all and I was terrified, but these men just looked at Fred as if he were crazy. Still, I will never forget his mannerisms, his sneer. I felt like garbage.

"Around this time, Uncle Fred introduced me to pornography, and some of it was pretty sophisticated stuff. I was fascinated and horrified by it. Whenever I found it (and eventually, I found where my dad's private 'library' was, too), I went though it and read it. It was exciting in some ways but so degrading that I felt contaminated. I hated myself for looking at it. I felt more ashamed of that than of the incest, because it was voluntary.

"By the time I was in high school, I had decided to become an artist. I wanted to illustrate children's books. But at home, in private, I drew male and female figures—adults and children—in sexual poses and situations. My mother found those drawings and that was devastating. She told me I was evil, perverted. I was embarrassed. I didn't understand why I was doing this. I had no models, the drawings were from memory. What I didn't realize was that I was drawing what had happened to me as well as things I had seen in pornographic material. It was, in a way, like art therapy.

"Later, when I was in art class and drawing fashion sketches, the teacher commented, 'Your models are so seductive!' Of course, the idea was to draw pictures resembling Vogue models and I was drawing something based on an entirely different magazine!

"By the time I was a sophomore, Fred and Marie had moved out. I had learned by then, however, that sex was part of the package with men. I wanted affirmation and validation and sex was required in order to get it. I was willing to pay the price. I slept with some boys, and I was raped at least twice.

"Meanwhile, it was getting worse at home. My father had moved from using his belt to his open hand to his fists. Eventually I left home and dropped out of school. I lived with some friends part of the time and on the streets part of the time." Pausing and shrugging, she said, "I only had one skill. I occasionally turned tricks for cash. My family found out—or just assumed—what was going on. They wrote me off as a whore.

"Things went on like this for six months. Finally, I went to my grandmother and asked for some help. We agreed that I could live rent-free at her apartment if I went to business school. The tuition would be a loan. Within a year, I had landed a secretarial job and was paying her back. I was finally a grown-up.

"That was so many years ago, but even picturing myself as an adolescent is painful. Of course, one look at my 13-year-old daughter, and I'm back in the middle of those feelings. I wish," she said and looked around at the sympathetic faces of the group, "I could look at her the way you are looking at me right now."

One of the critical elements of healing for Ruth and Gerri was having the support group listen to their stories with love and acceptance. Both of them had received a degrading type of "acceptance" based on someone's sexual use of their bodies. Within the support group, however, they could receive genuine affection and comfort.

An understanding spouse can also help by bringing this same ability to simply comfort and accept into the marital relationship. "After all these weeks, John and I finally made love a few days ago," Ruth said, "and afterward, I dissolved. I just started sobbing. At first, this look of terrible hurt crossed his face, but then he reached over and just wrapped me up in a blanket and rocked me in his arms."

Talking honestly about sexual experiences and feelings within a safe group is a good way to practice communication skills needed for a healthy adult sexual relationship. It is, of course, a radically different pattern from the sexual secret-keeping most incest survivors have learned.

Much of the help that the women in the group received was simply discovering that they were not alone in their struggle with the aftermath of traumatic sexualization as children. As Ruth told her story and listened to others, she realized that her curiosity about sex was natural, and given what was happening to her, absolutely predictable. The drawings that had caused her such embarrassment were indeed a form of art therapy and a poignant cry for help. Even her teenage experiences with casual sex and prostitution made sense given her limited understanding of the choices available to her.

Flashbacks and Fantasies

Telling the story is also a critical part of the healing process for an especially painful and typical problem: *flashbacks.* "My husband touched me gently on the neck the other night," Ruth said, "and suddenly I was in a cold sweat. For a moment I was convinced it was Uncle Fred and I remembered that whole scene at his brother's house. How are we ever going to have a normal life when my memories can reach out and paralyze me like this?"

Dr. Meiselman has suggested that much of the power of flashbacks lies in keeping them hidden. She notes that survivors can "wear out" the fear response of the flashback by talking about the memory again and again.[7]

This can be done with the therapist, with the support group, and in a personal journal. Eventually, the scene is so familiar, it no longer causes the same fearful response.

Another common problem with survivors is the recurrence of guilt-producing sexual fantasies. "It scares me that I have gotten aroused in the past thinking about rape or prostitution or being a child in a sexual situation," Gerri said quietly. "I worry that somehow that means it was my fault all of this happened to me."

It is not unusual for survivors to report that they get aroused by thinking about situations that are similar to the original abuse (for example, being with a much older partner; being talked into or forced to have sex). Since this is the way they were introduced to sexual feelings and contact, the response is not at all surprising, but it can make survivors feel tremendous guilt. As a result, they often immediately shut down their feelings, and lovemaking comes to a halt.

According to Meiselman, one of the most effective ways for survivors to deal with this response is to *increase* the number of fantasies they find pleasant. This does not even have to be limited to sexual situations, but can include pleasant settings (a deserted beach in the moonlight; a cabin in the mountains) or miraculous physical changes (Ruth's favorite: "I lose fifteen pounds instantly!"). When the guilt-producing fantasy arises, Meiselman noted, the survivor should not panic and berate herself, but gently turn her attention to an alternative fantasy.

Fantasy is, of course, part of sexual pleasure, an especially difficult area for survivors of sexual trauma. Oddly, this is true whether or not pleasure was part of their early experience. If the perpetrator (or perpetrators) had no concern at all about giving as well as receiving pleasure, survivors may assume sex is always painful and unpleasant. Survivors who did feel pleasure, however, may avoid sexual enjoyment because it brings up tremendous guilt over their childhood experience and response.

Sex is one area where experience—particularly traumatic childhood experience—is not always the best teacher. New behavior patterns must be learned and a new self-image built that includes a healthy sexuality and respect for the body.

Many survivors report a deep sense of shame or even hatred for their bodies. This can result in a split that distorts their perception of their physical selves. The same survivor can proclaim that she "never thinks of herself below the neck" and at another moment proclaim that she's "just a hole." Learning to enjoy physical pleasure of all types can be an important part of recovery in this important area. Several group members mentioned activities that gave them physical pleasure: (1) eating food slowly and consciously, (2) massage, (3) Jacuzzis, (4) bubble baths, (5) gentle exercise, (6) hugs, and (7) play ("I've taken my preschooler to the park four times this week," Ruth said, "I have to have some excuse for digging in the sandbox, right?").

Power and Sexuality

"The important thing for me in anything physical," Gerri said, "is that I have to be in control. For example, I only have my feet massaged—nothing else—because that is nonthreatening. It also feels great! But it is very important that I am the one that says this is what I want and this is what I don't want."

Setting these kinds of physical boundaries can be a life-changing experience for those whose boundaries were constantly violated in childhood. Many survivors report that they need to feel a sense of control before they can make love—even within a long-term and stable marriage. "I felt so weak and victimized with Uncle Fred," Ruth pointed out, "I really want to learn how to be sexual in a healthy way. Our therapist has suggested that John and I try an experiment for three weeks: I'm supposed to be the only one to suggest anything physical. This is not just making love—it can be hugging on the couch or going swimming. John has the option of accepting or turning me down or giving me a 'rain check' for later.

"John would tell you that nothing is going on, but I don't know—I think a lot is going on. Last night we took a shower together. I love having this much control. Power is kind of a turn-on!"

Alice looked at Ruth for a long moment. "Maybe that's what is wrong with my sex life," she said. "I sure know that I've *never* felt powerful."

Chapter 5

THE SURVIVOR AND POWER

"I never wanted to hurt anybody," Alice began slowly. It was a phrase she would repeat like a mantra at group sessions. "I just never was a fighter, even when I was little. My sisters would try to get to me and I would not fight. My oldest sister says I was the calmest, sweetest baby, real easy to take care of. I would let them hold me and I never cried or fussed. She says she still sees that patience in me."

Tracing the ridge of the chair with her fingernail, Alice paused for a long moment before adding, "And I've always been a victim."

The youngest of six children, Alice was still a toddler when her mother died. Moved back and forth between her father's home and the home of a series of relatives, she had had no time to develop a sense of control or choices. Other people's actions and needs always set the agenda. What she wanted or needed never seemed to matter.

When she was 5 years old, her 11-year-old brother David pulled her into the bedroom whispering, "I want to show you something, I want to show you something!" He had her lay down on the bed and part her legs.

"I was only 5," she said, "and I didn't have any idea what he was doing. I thought it was a game." David had begun to penetrate her when her father burst into the room. A Methodist lay preacher with a violent temper, her father began to scream, "You *devils!* You are *Satan!* I will beat the evil right out of you!"

Pulling David off the bed, he made the boy kneel as he took off his belt. Alice watched in terror as her father began to beat her brother, using the large metal buckle to inflict bruises all over the upper part of his body. As the belt fell, her father repeated, "You are a devil and I will kill you!" He began to lash David across the head and Alice screamed as the blood poured down his face.

"I thought he was killing David," she said. "It certainly looked as if he were going to die. I screamed, 'Don't kill my brooo-ther." As she told the story, Alice's eyes widened and filled with tears and her voice became the weak, high-pitched wail of a little girl.

What did her father do to her? "I can't remember," she sobbed, "I can't remember what happened after that. I can just see David and I hear myself and I can't remember. I just know that whatever it is—whatever he did—it has made me inorgasmic. I have never— never—had a positive sexual experience with a man."[1]

Trying to Stay Alive

The combination of sexual trauma and a domineering father who alternated between beating his children and ignoring or abandoning them, convinced Alice that she had no choice at all. She was trapped.

"Reading *The Color Purple* was like looking in a mirror for me," Alice said. "Remember when Celie's sister asks her why she doesn't fight back against her husband and she says 'But I don't know how to fight. All I know how to do is stay alive'? I cried when I read that. I'm always trying to please; trying to keep out of the way."

Alice's survival was as hard to come by as Celie's. When she was 8, her father remarried and moved with the oldest children to California. Alice and an older sister were left with their maternal grandmother. One day a friend of her sister's, a 15-year-old boy named Toby, took Alice with him on a bicycle ride. Toby's brother Sam, who was 10, came alone with them on another bike.

"We came to a field," Alice told the group, "And Toby told me to lay down on the ground." She paused for a moment. "I trusted him. I did what he asked."

Toby jumped on top of her and began to rape her. When Alice cried, Toby's brother began to get upset. "Stop! Stop! You're hurting her!" the younger boy insisted, but Toby continued to try to penetrate her for several minutes.

After the boys left, the little girl walked home alone. She never told anyone what happened and while the rape had caused her intense physical pain, she felt she was to blame. "Until that happened," Alice explained, "I liked him touching me. You know, just sitting on the bike with him, riding. My father had left us. My grandmother didn't seem to have enough time or food for us. I thought Toby was nice."

Before adulthood, Alice would be raped again twice. Both times they were surprise attacks. One was a date, the second a stranger. Both times the men terrified her simply by pushing her roughly and telling her to shut up. She did not get angry at the men. She never told. "I knew nobody would believe me," she explained.

Learned Helplessness

People who have had healthy childhoods emerge with a sense of mastery and self-confidence. They watch as their actions have an impact on others and they learn about choices. The key element of self-esteem, however, has little opportunity to develop in an abusive home. What may develop instead is a child's conviction that she has no power to direct her own life. Martin Seligman's study on "learned helplessness" provides a theoretical model for this response:

> Seligman's . . . research team placed dogs in cages and administered electrical shocks at random and varied intervals. The dogs quickly learned that no matter what response they made, they could not control the shock. In the beginning, the dogs tried various movements in an attempt to escape. When nothing they did stopped the shocks, they ceased any voluntary action and became submissive. Later the researchers changed the procedure and attempted to teach the dogs that they could escape by crossing to the other side of the cage, but the dogs still remained passive and helpless. Even when the door was left open and the dogs were shown the way out, they refused to leave and did not avoid the shock.
>
> The earlier in life the dogs received such treatment, the longer it took to overcome the effects of this so-called learned helplessness.[2]

When a child's life is as unpredictable and as filled with physical and emotional shock as Alice's, she is robbed not only of present choices but also of the sense of power she will need to make future ones. As a female, her helplessness will be reinforced by most cultural models of femininity (particularly within the conservative Christian community) which emphasize submission and deference over strength and decisiveness. Finally, if a girl's own mother is a woman who avoids making decisions or is unable to protect her children, it will be even more difficult for the child to believe that women have choices.

For Alice, the terrible loss of her mother was complicated by a deeply held fantasy image of motherhood, a picture that left little room for personal choices or the expression of anger. "I was 2-1/2 when my mother died," Alice noted. "She was like everything they tell you about Mary, the mother of Jesus. My brothers and sisters tell me she never got mad and she was always loving. She cared for us and would do anything for her children."

This passive picture of Mary was a great comfort to a little girl who wanted a mother who never got mad (unlike her abusive relatives) and who loved her no matter what. At the same time, however, this fantasy image reinforced Alice's belief that anger at others was not an emotion women—especially Christian women— were allowed to have. Her rage at years of bad treatment was forced down and, with nowhere else to go, turned inward with a vengeance. At the age of 18, Alice was hospitalized for depression after an almost-successful suicide attempt. "I had no self-esteem. None. It did not matter if I lived. I wanted to die," she remembered.

A few years later, Alice met and married a man from her church, convinced that having a family of her own would heal her depression permanently. They had three children in the next five years. This young woman, who had never made choices for herself, suddenly had three small lives to protect and guide. She found it overwhelming and she asked the doctor for a tubal ligation. "I couldn't handle more children and I was afraid of hurting the ones I had," she said. An unforeseen series of complications eventually required her to undergo a complete hysterectomy.

Released from the hospital, she went home and slipped back into a deep depression. "I wanted to live for my babies," Alice said. "I knew my babies needed me. I would tell myself I had to live to see them grow up, because I knew how hard it had been on me when my mother died when I was 2-1/2. But when I made my second suicide attempt, my youngest girl was just," she said thoughtfully, "well, she would have been about 2-1/2 years old."

Although depression was a constant companion, Alice did not attempt to take her life again until she was 45. It was about this time that Alice's brother David died of cirrhosis of the liver, the result of alcoholism that had begun in his teens. "I went to his funeral wearing bandages on both my wrists. My husband had found me unconscious on the bathroom floor and rushed me to the hospital. I leaned down close to my brother's face when I got to the casket, 'It should have been me, David,' I told him.

"You know," Alice said, "after that terrible beating I always felt protective toward him. David was the artistic one in our family. He had a wonderful visual memory and fine drawing ability, but he never had the chance to make anything of it.

"I cried all the way home. I knew that memory had chased David into a bottle and an early grave. I had to try to beat it. I had to find help. One dead body was enough for this family to sacrifice. When I got home, I made an appointment with a therapist." For the first time, Alice chose life for herself. Not for her babies. Not

for her husband. For Alice. It was a first—but critical—
step away from helplessness. She and her therapist
became partners in discovering and affirming the Inner
Child crushed by years of abuse.

Anger: Sinful or Godly?

Six years later, Alice joined the support group for
adults molested as children. It was especially important
to her that this was a church-based group. "My therapist
has helped my self-esteem a lot," Alice told the group,
"But she isn't a Christian. She wants me to talk about
my anger and she doesn't seem to understand that I've
forgiven everyone of my abusers in Jesus' name."

It was soon apparent that Alice had two convictions
about anger: anger is uncontrollable, and anger is sinful.
When people in the group shared their pain, Alice
found it easy to support them. When they expressed
their rage at their victimization, however, she was visibly
uncomfortable. "I never wanted to hurt anybody"
became a nervous refrain. Alice's earliest experiences
had convinced her that anger ended in terrible abuse of
others and if she ever really got angry, she would not be
able to control it. Her father had never been able to
control his rage. The man she had dated—one of the
men who raped her—had been controlled by his anger.
In fact, Alice's greatest inner fear was that someday,
inevitably, her anger would burst forth and turn her into
a monster.

For Alice, learning how to get angry without abusing
others was a new experience. With the support of the
group, she took very small steps toward facing this part
of herself. One evening she told the group about her

employer's rude treatment of her. Suddenly, she picked up the Kleenex box beside her and sent if flying into a corner. The group broke into applause and laughter. It was a step out of Alice's cage of "learned helplessness," and other than slightly crumpling a cardboard box of tissues, her anger had not resulted in anything harmful. Struggling with appropriate ways to express anger responsibly is a central issue for survivors. Part of the issue is practical: learning effective methods for controlling and dealing with anger. Part of the issue is theoretical: giving oneself permission to have feelings.

St. Paul told his followers to "be angry and sin not. Let not the sun go down on your wrath (Eph. 4:26)." This is the ideal way to handle anger—immediately, or at least within a twenty-four hour period. This is the goal for true mental and spiritual health. Face your anger as soon as possible, admit the cause, and confront and resolve the situation in a healthy way.

This method is diametrically opposed to the way survivors of dysfunctional families had to deal with anger. Admitting anger can be dangerous—even life-threatening—in abusive situations. In Alice's case, many suns had set during the years in which she had desperately pushed her rage deeper and deeper within herself. She longed to resolve these feelings, but years of built-up anger cannot be processed quickly. Just as in Seligman's experiments, the earlier in life consistent mistreatment occurs, the harder it is to change patterns.

When Anger Reveals Hatred

In the safety of the group, Alice began admitting her rage at the many people who had abandoned her intentionally (her abusive father) and inadvertently (her saintly mother). Soon, however, she was terrified at the specter of a new rage-linked emotion: hatred. "Christians are not supposed to hate—not even their enemies. We are supposed to honor our parents. We should forgive everyone, no matter what. I can't pray or feel like a Christian when I talk about hating people," she insisted through tears.

For victims of sexual abuse like Alice, memories of being humiliated, hurt, ignored, and betrayed stir up a deep sense of hatred against the people who were actively and passively involved in the abuse. This response to unjust and cruel treatment is normal.

Can hatred, however, be integrated not only with emotional health, but also with faith and spiritual health? It is true that Scripture exhorts us to love our enemies, yet when we feel anger and hate and we open our mouths to pray, it is not with love. The good news is that *we do not have to wait until we love our enemies to pray.* There are biblical prayers for those in the grip of rage and hatred. Here is just one example: "O Daughter of Babylon, doomed to destruction, happy is he who repays you for what you have done to us—he who seizes your infants and dashes them against the rocks" (Ps. 137:8–9).

It would have been sinful, of course, for the enraged Israelites crying out in this psalm to have actually killed Babylonian babies. That is not the point. This prayer reflects the anguish of Jewish parents who had seen their children kidnapped, enslaved, or murdered in Babylonian raids on their nation. Many people are uncomfortable reading this testimony to ugly emotions within Scripture, but it is there (along with many similar passages) for a reason. God can hear and honor anguished prayers. God holds us responsible for our action but has compassion for our pain.

As Alice experienced that compassion, her terror lessened. Over the next weeks, she was even able to examine her insistence that she "never wanted to hurt anyone." In fact, she had tried repeatedly to hurt her own Inner Child. Several suicide attempts showed the depths of her murderous rage. Eventually, Alice admitted that over the last two decades she had been physically abusive to her children on several occasions.

"The reason I decided to have a tubal ligation was because I was so afraid I would hurt the children. The day I called the doctor for the appointment, I hit my son so hard he flew against the wall. He looked up at me—terrified. I thought, 'I'm turning into my father.'"

"It was about that time," Alice told the group, "that I began to have a recurring dream. I am on an escalator, going down and down and down for miles. I begin to get scared. Then suddenly I reach the end of the escalator and walk out into a basement. I can feel myself sinking down and starting to crawl on all fours. I am making these ugly sounds. I realize with horror that I have become a groaning, growling monster. At that moment a ghost enters the room and tries to kill me. That is when I always wake up. Often my children have come in and awakened me from my sleep at this point because I moan so loudly!

"A few days ago I realized that the 'monster' was my anger! I was going deeper into my unconscious and discovering a side of myself that felt ugly. It was a monster I wanted to kill."

Morton Kelsey has said that when we turn inward

with honesty, we confront the "inner murderer." "I have come to trust only those people who are aware of their inner murderer. I have come to trust only those people who are aware of their inner rage, of the inner murderers within them capable of murdering me. Only those who know the capacity to destroy can keep it in hand and deter it."[3]

Taming the inner murderer was not an easy task for Alice. Once she had acknowledged her anger, learning to express it appropriately was difficult. "I choke up or cry or I say something I am sorry for later," she said. "Sometimes I feel like I am about two years old."

Expressing her feelings in a journal provided a "safe" way to explore her rage, and she often wrote compulsively for hours. One evening, Alice told the group, "I had my monster dream again this week, but the ghost did not try to kill me. I woke up naturally. I think it means that I have stopped trying to kill my anger." Eventually, she began to see anger as her friend, a "red alert" that signalled something was wrong. Rather than suppressing her rage or giving in to it, she could make choices to change the situation.

The group were vocal cheerleaders as Alice worked through her anger at others and at her own inner murderer. Sharing with God all of their rage and hurt, however, soon led to a new problem. "I'm angry at *God*," Sharon told the group. "Just how am I supposed to pray about that?"

Chapter 6

THE SURVIVOR AND PRAYER

"Every night I prayed, 'If there is a God in heaven, please let him intervene tonight,'" Sharon remembered. "Please don't let my father come in,' I'd say, 'Please kill him; please do something; just get him out of my life. Don't let this happen.'" Looking up from her prayers, Sharon would see the huge figure standing in the doorway and know that there would be no rescue tonight.

Rick, the man in the doorway, believed he had a right to anything—and anyone—he wanted in that house. A 220-pound amateur weight lifter, he didn't find it hard to get his way with his shy, soft-spoken wife or their four young children.

Professionally, Rick was known as a brilliant if taciturn man. One of the top "fly-boys" in the Air Force during the Korean War, he had gone on to be a test pilot. Veteran's benefits put him through graduate school and eventually he became a physics, aviation, and mathematics professor at a state college. However, chronic health problems plagued Rick and his wife Grace; in one year the two of them had a total of seven operations and the absences from work and mounting bills resulted in several job changes.

In between were several long stints of unemployment.

During those times, Grace would take a night job so that her husband could look for work during the day and they would not have to hire a babysitter. During the evenings, Rick was in charge of the children. It was during the first of these stretches of unemployment that he began to escalate from verbal bullying to beating the children. Grace saw the welts and bruises but never dared to confront her husband.

At that point, Rick got an aircraft engineering job that required a move to California. "I was 12 years old the year we moved," Sharon said. "We had not been in the new house long when my father asked my mother, 'Have you talked to her about menstruation yet?' My mother—a very shy, sheltered woman—blushed and said no, and she looked upset. Then my father said, 'Well, I'm taking over.'

"He supposedly would have 'talks' with me in the bedroom but in fact, he was molesting me. I would try to signal my mother that I did not *want* to talk anymore but she would just bite her lip and put her head down. She was not able to fight him. She didn't really know what was going on but she didn't *want* to know either.

"Then several weeks later, the aircraft company my father worked for put him on a newly started rocket program. He had to go through a security clearance and he was so uptight about that. The tension was building at home. All of the children were getting kicked and beaten. It was during this time that he first attacked me and raped me. I was still just 12 years old. After that, the rapes happened about once a week for over two years. It hurt, but he would put a pillow over my mouth so that no one would hear me crying.

"I started a few times to tell my mother in different

ways. The problem was that she was such a naive person. She did not seem to be able to imagine what I was trying to tell her."

So, instead of pursuing a topic that made her uncomfortable, Sharon's mother simply dropped the subject. Then when Sharon was fifteen, her mother took another night job. With his wife away at work Rick started coming to his daughter's bed every night.

How Can God Allow This?

One question comes up again and again in support groups for the survivors of sexual abuse: How could God let this horror happen to a child? For women and men who desire spiritual growth, the question can become an overwhelming roadblock. Faith becomes an absurdity. Prayer becomes impossible.

Is reframing one's view of God critical to healing? We believe it is. Certainly, survivors of sexual abuse feel a profound sense of loss over their shattered concept of God, of faith, and of life's meaning. Sexual abuse is not, of course, the only cause of spiritual trauma. Life in the real world forces all of us into encounters with evil that have an enormous impact on our spiritual and emotional lives.

Carl Jung, referring to the Protestant, Jewish, and Catholic clients he had treated over the years, boldly linked their emotional turmoil to their spiritual loss: "It is safe to say that everyone of them fell ill because he had lost that which the living religions of every age have given to their followers, and none of them has been really healed who did not regain his religious outlook."[1]

Survivors cannot regain a healthy spiritual outlook,

however, until they understand how the abuse they experienced gave them distorted messages about God, about life, and about spiritual truth. The biblical picture of a God who is good, loving, powerful, and a perfect spiritual parent is a doctrine all Christians share. These basic and foundational messages, however, are attacked and damaged by child sexual abuse. The chart on the next page shows the direct link exists between the sexual violation of the child and the violation of faith.

All four of the trauma-causing factors of child sexual abuse discussed in Chapter 1 that so deeply distort the child's self-image also cut the child off from a healthy spiritual outlook, in the following ways:

1. The *stigmatization* of a victim is convincing evidence that God (like everyone else) does not accept or love her. How can she pray when she is isolated and shamed?

2. The sense of *powerlessness* she feels at her abuse distorts her concept of a sovereign God. How can a child have confidence in an all-powerful God who did not rescue her?

3. The *betrayal* of incest strikes at the heart of a belief in God's righteousness. How can a child believe in a good God when she has been unfairly victimized by evil?

4. The *traumatic sexualization* of the child changes all of her messages about gender, sexuality, and parenting. How can a child feel cherished by a Parent God when she was molested—particularly if the perpetrator was her father or mother?

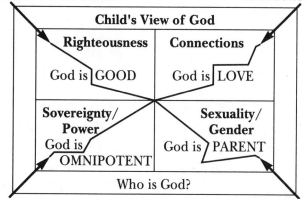

STIGMATIZATION
Response: God has abandoned me!

BETRAYAL
Response: God is unfair!

POWERLESSNESS
Response: God did not rescue me!

TRAUMATIC SEXUALIZATION
Response: God is just like the abuser!

Figure 3. Child Sexual Abuse: Impact on the Child's View of God

The spiritual feelings that the experience evokes are turbulent. The child's God-concept has been highly influenced by abuse and the result is a very real fear and perhaps even hatred. The survivor's choice is either to suppress those feelings—and settle for a numbed soul cut off from spiritual reality—or to explore the sorrow and anger and hatred that lurk below the surface.

Praying to a God We Hate

How shall we pray when it is *God* whom we hate? Can we pray such heresy? Yes. In fact, the only beginning for an authentic relationship with God is to express that anguish openly. Reading a hundred books on the nature of God will never erase the inner twisting of a survivor's view of God. Ignoring the anger within—or "correcting" it—cannot build a legitimate faith. Only a personal relationship based on honest prayer can start the spiritual healing. Facing and grieving over the anger, the hatred, and the profound loss is the secret to spiritual liberation. In his extremely helpful book *May I Hate God?*, Pierre Wolff tells the following story:

I can still hear the retreatant repeating three times before me, "God, I hate you because you let this happen." I still see her letting go of her tension because I did not pronounce any judgment, because the sky did not fall on her head.

When it is possible to speak a word, it liberates. We do not always remember that it is precisely a word, a Word articulated in our flesh, which has liberated us.[2]

It is not wrong to tell God what we really feel. It is the first step of true faith. For the victim of sexual abuse, it is freedom from bondage to an ugly secret. Should we love God? Yes, but Scripture shows us that *we do not have to wait until we love God to pray.*

Not every angry prayer, however, is healing. To be effective in building spiritual health, the expressions of hurt and anger must be as *clear and specific* as possible. That is not easy for most survivors. People who were raised in dysfunctional families don't have healthy patterns for expressing anger. One young woman, encouraged by a support leader to express her feelings directly to God, responded by cussing out the Almighty with a string of four-letter words. Her courage and desire to communicate with God were real, but the prayer was abusive rather than healing. In this woman's family, anger was only expressed through cursing, name-calling, and violence. For her, learning how to be angry with God—or with anyone else—*without* becoming abusive was the first lesson in prayer.

This does not mean that we have to tiptoe around our anger or adopt a phony sweetness in talking to God when we are hurting. Prayer only has power when we tell the truth. Scripture shows us that effective prayers require a painfully honest baring of the soul; such prayers are not always "nice" or even "reverent."

Here are three liberating scriptural prayers that give us new models for expressing emotions to God.

Liberating Prayer #1: God, you are unfair and unfaithful!

Most of us believe that God is (or should be) in the business of rewarding the righteous and punishing the wicked. When our life experience dashes those expectations, we feel cheated. Yet, the testimony of Scripture is that committed servants of the Lord often feel unrewarded. "Why do you treat your servant so badly?" Moses cried (Num. 11:11). The Reverend Marie Wiebe, a Covenant pastor, says she has her own version of Moses' prayer. Driving alone in her car, she has prayed aloud in exasperation, "Do you know how hard it is to work for you, God?"

When God seems to move too slowly to show gratitude to those who are on the right side, we become discouraged. However, when evil triumphs completely, we feel betrayed. How can we pray to a sovereign God when the innocent suffer and the guilty benefit?

Sharon's world as a teenager was ruled by her tyrant

father who seemed to gather all the benefits while the children only suffered. By the time she was 15, Sharon explained, "My father was also sexually abusing both of my younger sisters. He had not raped them yet but he was dragging them off to the bedroom at night to molest them. The physical abuse was constant—he was especially cruel to my brother. Then he started molesting my brother as well.

"Despite all the abuse, my father always acted like Mr. Righteous. He was a church member and one day the local minister came and was just charmed with my father and his pious talk. I wanted to scream, 'Can't you see through him?' But no one did. Dad was always preaching at us about fire and brimstone. And he was big on what he saw as his biblical privileges as the 'man of the house.' He made sure we knew all about *those* scriptures."

"Why do you reward the wicked?" the Psalmist asks. That was also Sharon's question as she wondered how a righteous God could give this man all of those privileges and give her so much undeserved pain.

Liberating Prayer #2: God, you are responsible for my pain! You withhold rescue, indeed you destroy me!

Sharon's nightly prayers for rescue became more desperate. Maybe tonight, she would think, God will answer my prayer. "Don't let this happen! Don't let this happen!' I would whisper. I would stand on my head—literally—and pray this prayer to God because I figured, if he isn't going to listen to me upright on my knees, he's going to listen to me on my head! He's *gotta* listen!"

Every night, however, was the same. The rapes continued.

Unrescued and apparently unheard, Sharon in her heart echoed this ancient prayer of Job's:

I loathe my very life; therefore I will give free rein to my complaint and speak out in the bitterness of my soul. I will say to God: Do not condemn me, but tell me what charges you have against me. Does it please you to oppress me, to spurn the work of your hands, while you smile on the schemes of the wicked? Do you have eyes of flesh? Do you see as a mortal sees? . . . . Your hands shaped me and made me. Will you now turn and destroy me? . . . . Why then did you bring me out of the womb? I wish I had died before any eye saw me. (Job 10:1–4, 8, 18)

Liberating Prayer #3: God, you have abandoned me and left me utterly alone!

Unlike most sexually abused children, Sharon took the risk of talking about her father's assaults to three adults: a teacher, a school guidance counselor, and a neighbor. The counselor refused to believe her. The teacher dismissed her with a laugh. The neighbor phoned Sharon's father, who denied everything and beat his daughter unmercifully that night.

Then Sharon's friend Beth—who lived in another city—came over to spend the weekend. Rick made several sexual passes at her. Beth returned home and told her mother about Rick's behavior and about her suspicions regarding Sharon's predicament. Beth's mother phoned the Schultz home late that Monday night. When he got off the phone, Rick went directly into Sharon's room. "He grabbed a pillow and he started to smother me. I suddenly realized that he was trying to keep me from breathing but not leave any bruises—he didn't want to go to jail for murder. The phone call had convinced him that I was a threat to his safety. He was trying to kill me and cover it up. I was furious. I kneed him in the groin.

"Remember, I was not quite 16 and pretty little. We are talking about a 130-pound difference in body weight! This was the first time I had tried to fight my father physically and the surprise—as well as the pain—sent him reeling. I pushed him away and ran into the bathroom, which was right off the bedroom, and locked the door. Then he got up and tried to break the door down.

"By this time, my two sisters and brother were awake. My brother didn't really know what to do. He was small for his age and he had been savagely beaten by my father before. So my youngest sister—who was 12—ran into the kitchen and got the biggest butcher knife she could find. Then she went up to our father with fire in her eyes (my other sister says she will never forget that look) and said, 'Leave her alone or I will kill you.' Dad stared at her and when he backed off, she shouted, 'Sharon, come out!'

"So I came out and I ran. I went out of the door and I ran as hard as I could. I was worried about the three other kids but I figured they would be safe as long as she had the knife. Also, I could run the distance—a mile and a half—to the nearest county sheriff's station in fifteen minutes and I knew it. By that time, my father had gotten into his car and was chasing me but he couldn't come down the alleys and across the railroad tracks and through the field like I could. So he turned the car around and headed home."

Finally, the shivering teenager—still dressed in her nightgown—reached the station. "Look, I need to get out of the house," Sharon told the officer. "I'll go anywhere; put me in a safe place. Put me in a foster home, just get me away from there and take my sisters and my brother." Deputy Smith listened to the story of nightly sexual assaults. "He didn't say much; I was crying and crying. Finally he told me, 'You wait here for a few minutes and compose yourself. I'll go and get a reporter and you can tell the story again so we can get you to the right channels.' Well, little did I realize that he called both my parents (reaching my mother at work). When I told the story again they were in the next room listening in on the intercom. That was the first time my mother heard the story, and my father was vehemently denying everything."

When Sharon finished her story the officer opened the door to the other room and the girl stared in shock at Rick and Grace Schultz. The officer closed his notepad and walked over to the parents. "If she were my daughter," he said coldly, "I would take her home and spank her."

There are so many reasons for an adult to ignore a hurting child. Even children who—like Sharon—have physical signs of cruel physical abuse and traumatic rape are often dismissed back to the custody of their tormentors. For the child who is the victim of a more typical type of sexual abuse (which involved neither violence nor penetration), there is usually no medical evidence to force adults to pay attention. Even with the growing technology of detection, many types of sexual abuse leave few physical indicators.[3]

The sad truth is that most adults will not take the risk

of protecting a child from family members, especially if the child appears to be physically healthy. As Dr. Roland Summit has said, we tend to believe that a child was sexually abused only after we find her discarded body in a trash dumpster.

But for every headline about the discovery of another small abused corpse, there are hundreds of children who are unmarked and well dressed who carry a painful and isolating secret. They know that telling the truth will get them into serious trouble. Who would believe that a "nice person" (like the neighbor or the coach or their uncle) would sexually harass a child? These children feel used and powerless. They feel guilty and ashamed. The years pass and the children become adults, but healing eludes them. As silenced and alone in life as other victims have been in death, they pray with Jesus, "My God, my God, *why* have you abandoned me?" (Mark 15:34).

A wordless form of Jesus' prayer of abandonment formed in Sharon's mind as she stood, tearstained and shaking, before Deputy Smith. The rage at this latest betrayal suddenly gave her new determination. "I won't go back with them," she told him evenly. "I am pressing charges."

"My mother looked at me with shock. She was humiliated. 'If you'll just come home, I'll make sure you are okay,' she told me. 'I don't believe that,' I said, 'You never made sure before! I am going to call Bill.'

"Bill was my high school boyfriend. He was real nice but dumb, dumb, dumb! I used to write his English papers for him so that he could pass. Still, he was in love with me and so sweet: my protector! When I phoned, his mother said I could come and stay at their house for a while. For the first time since my little sister had helped me escape, I wasn't facing this alone. My father and mother were so shaken that they agreed."

In fact, the confrontation had finally pushed Rick over the edge. "When my parents got home," Sharon said, "my mother went to the other kids and got their side of the story. She looked at my father and demanded, 'Now Rick, what is going on?' At that point, my father turned white, fell like he was going into a coma, and curled up in the fetal position." Grace called the paramedics and had her husband hospitalized. The diagnosis was schizophrenia.

Rick's psychotic break was probably as important as the children's depositions (only Sharon and her youngest sister testified against their father) in convincing the court to find him guilty of child sexual abuse. Rick was sentenced to a state hospital for the criminally insane. After two years, however, his doctors recommended his release and he eventually got another good job in the aerospace industry. By then, however, the marriage to Grace had ended. Rick went on to remarry three times, each time choosing a woman who had children.

Sharon, meanwhile, was free of the oppressor who had tried to take her life, but the ache of feeling abandoned by God throbbed on for years. Sometimes she tried to pray the words she heard in church, but they seemed to hit the ceiling and break into pieces. For years, she simply gave up on prayers at all.

Twenty-five years down the road, however, after she had entered therapy and had begun to explore her painful memories, prayers again sprang to her lips: prayers like the ones from her anguished childhood, like the laments of the Psalmist, the accusations of Job, and the dying cry of Jesus Christ.

Reasons to Pray Honestly

How can we dare to pray such terrible prayers? Ironically, for those who were sexually abused in ways less physically traumatic then Sharon's abuse, allowing themselves to pray out their rage may be even more difficult.

Even admitting those feelings may be overwhelming. After all, these victims point out, "My life wasn't in danger. He never hurt me"; "I felt too embarrassed to tell anyone, so it is probably my fault it didn't stop"; "I never had the courage to run away"; "I used to accept his bribes—use the sex to get what I needed"; "He wasn't insane; in fact, I may be the crazy one."

While Sharon had the support of her siblings, (the belated) support of a court judgment, and her father's obvious mental illness to prove that she had been wronged, most other children had far less to connect them with this reality. They assume "I did not deserve a rescue." They minimize their plight. They swallow—and deny—their anger at a God who is pictured as a loving, powerful, righteous parent, and they lose their connection with this God. Feeling unworthy to mourn and accuse, they slip back into spiritual isolation and masquerading.

Can people who feel so unworthy (whether they were the victims of sexual abuse or some other type of hurt) dare to pray such terrible prayers? Yes. The first reason they can take this spiritual risk is that *God is indeed fair and faithful and will not turn away from us in our pain.*

God does not wait for our love but first loves us. God does not wait for our theology to be correct but asks for our honest feelings.

When Job was bold enough to hold God responsible for his suffering, God did not punish him. In fact, it was Job's friends—pious frauds mouthing spiritual clichés—who aroused the Almighty's wrath. Job's audacity was straight from the heart. It was an act of faith and love. He told God the truth. It is this telling the truth about the evil and unjust suffering in the world that is the beginning of spiritual health. The Bible does not present a Hallmark edition of life on earth. The pain, the cruelty, and the sin of humanity are established facts from Genesis onward. Not only does Scripture insist that sin and evil are real but also specifically warns that the innocent are often the victims of that evil.

Today's Church often makes the mistake of ignoring evil or at least of implying that Christians are immune to it. This is dangerous theology. The reality of child sexual abuse forces us into a far more biblical world view. We must tell the truth about what we see and experience.

This brings us to the second reason we can pray honestly: *a loving God is safe to talk to and will not destroy us when we admit our rage at our fate.* God allows us to walk through our anger and hatred as a bridge to the acceptance of divine love.

Imagine a small child, a toddler, furious and hurt. She knows her mother could give her the desire of her heart and cannot understand why she is being denied. Crying, she insists, "I *hate* you, Mommy!" The wise mother does not argue. She knows that her child does indeed "hate" her at that moment and she understands and feels the child's frustration. She says nothing, or perhaps she says only, "Yes, I know." The small fists beat against her for a moment, the eyes shut tight. "I hate you, I hate you!" Then the small head drops, the hands relax, and the tears of sorrow begin. It is at this moment that the child knows that it is the parent who is in charge, and who will not yield her leadership even to tears. Even more important, the little girl discovers that her parent loves her enough to tolerate a confession of the most frightening feelings a child can have.

This is not a situation every daughter identifies with—those feelings are only safe to admit when we are loved. In the same way, we can only admit those terrible feelings when we really believe we are safe with God, when we believe in that love even though we are at our most unlovely.

If you can rage at God in safety; if you can admit your anger, your grief, your depression; if you believe in a Lord who allows such honesty, you possess profound trust.

This is what faith in God looks like.

Finally, we can pray our feelings of abandonment with honesty because *we are not alone*. This is in contrast to the view many of us have of a Christian reality that isolates those in pain.

The typical "chain of command" picture places God at the top of every hierarchy of power. Thus God is followed

- in the home, by the husband, the wife, and finally, the children;

- in the economy, by the rich, the middle class, and finally, the poor and homeless;

- in society, by the employer, then the employee, and ultimately the slave;

- in the legal system, by the judge, the police, law-abiding citizens, and finally the criminal;

- in the church, by the clergy and to a lesser extent by the devout, while the godless are excluded from blessing and authority.

The problem with all of these systems is the same. The oppressed and abused person feels at the bottom of each of these hierarchies, far from God. She is the child, the homeless, the slave, the criminal. She feels godless and alone. It is to this person that the words and actions of Jesus are especially sweet. Jesus insisted that in his kingdom, "The first shall be last and the last shall be first."

In Christ's revolutionary economy, it was not the male head of the household, but the child who represented God ("for of such is the kingdom of heaven"). He shunned the religious people and dined with the godless. He blessed the poor, touched the leper, and warned of the dangers of riches and position. He called himself a servant and died identified as a criminal. Rather than representing a God who moves primarily through the powerful and identifies with the strong, Jesus is the picture of a God who stands with the weak. In Christ's predictions about the final judgment, it is not how respectfully we have treated those in authority that will prove our godliness. Our spiritual life, according to Matthew 25:31–46, will be evaluated by how we have treated the people at the bottom of the social ladder: the poor, the abandoned, the weak.

The German pastor Dietrich Bonhoeffer watched evil devour the innocent as he sat imprisoned in a Nazi concentration camp. There, he penned the following poignant description of Christianity. (Although Bonhoeffer uses the term *men,* *women* and especially *children* could be substituted.)

"Christians and Pagans"

Men go to God when they are sore bestead,
Pray to him for succor, for his peace, for bread,
For mercy for them sick, sinning, or dead;
All men do so, Christian and unbelieving.

Men go to God when he is sore bestead,
Find him poor and scorned, without shelter or bread,
Whelmed under weight of the wicked, the weak,
    the dead;
Christians stand by God in his hour of grieving.

God goes to every man when sore bestead,
Feeds body and spirit with his bread;
For Christians, pagans, alike he hangs dead,
and both alike forgiving.[4]

Where is Jesus when a child is in pain? Jesus is the child. To serve that child is to serve Christ. "If you have done it onto the *least* of these," Christ insisted, "you have done it onto me" (Matt. 25:40). It is this Jesus who is with all victims, whether the hurts are sexual, physical, emotional, or spiritual. He prays a terrible prayer with us: "My God, my God, why have you abandoned me?" He will not leave us alone in our desperate need.

Chapter 7

THE SURVIVOR AND GOD

Once prayer has been reclaimed, a new issue is raised for many people overcoming childhood trauma. Who is it that we pray to? The most popular name for God in our culture is God the Father. This name sets off internal alarms, however, for the person who was abused by her father. As Sharon explained, "It is really hard to accept a heavenly Father when you've hated your real father and have not been able to trust him. When the only father that you ever had used and betrayed you, how can you expect this guy upstairs to do good things for you?"

God as Parent is the most difficult spiritual concept for survivors to repair. This is true for all children who were abused, even when the abuser is outside of the family but has had an important position of authority over the child. When an adult is sexual with a child, the experience sends a twofold message that says (1) people in authority use you, and (2) all relationships can be sexualized.

God, You Are Just Like My Abuser!

For the child who was abused by her father, however, the issue is especially explosive. The child who is from a healthy home finds the picture of God the Father rich and beautiful. Jesus urged us to come to this Spiritual Parent as full of trust as a well-loved child. This is a God you can call "Abba" (or "Dada"), Christ told us. Sadly, this comforting message is distorted by the experience of father-daughter incest. "God is just like my father" is a horrifying concept for those who had abusive parents.

"Yesterday," Donna told the support group, "I drove home from my therapist's office and the memories kept flooding back. I couldn't stop crying. I told God, 'I hate you for being a man! I hate you for being a *father*! I know what fathers do to daughters!'

"I just can't pray the Lord's Prayer anymore. I can't get past the connection in my mind between the word *father* and abusive sex. If I think of God the Father, I think of a man with a penis."

Most survivors do not express the issue as graphically (or poignantly) as Donna, but the troubling connection between their view of the abuser, their view of sex, and their view of God remains for them all. The appropriate sexual boundaries for parent-child relationships were destroyed and since God is the original Parent, *even the relationship with God seems potentially abusive and sexual to the survivor.* The concept of God has been traumatically sexualized in a very literal way. No matter how much lip service a survivor gives to the concept of God the Father, no matter how many bible studies she attends, the image can have an emotional impact that quite simply brings prayer and a sense of spiritual security to at least a temporary halt.

The emphasis within the Church upon God as male parent is so pervasive, however, that it is hard to escape. Actress and survivor Roberta Nobleman writes:

Church? Yes, I was sent to Sunday School. My mother went to church occasionally, my father never, but there I learned of a God who was also called Father, and I wasn't sure that I could trust Him either because I *was* sure that what Dad and I did in secret was dirty and wrong and that it "incurred God's wrath and indignation against me." I used to have some comfort from a statue of Mary, and I was envious of my Roman Catholic cousins because their church was always full of candles and incense and seemed so much more feminine. I remember looking longingly at those boxes that said "Confession," wishing my church provided a little quiet place where you could "go tell." I know now, of course, that the average Confessor of any denomination would be totally nonplussed in dealing with a little girl and her story of sexual abuse. And how do you tell father about father? He will probably tell you to confess it all to Father.[1]

If a little girl were mauled by a circus lion, few of us would insist that she think of God as a strong lion, although that is a biblical image of God used in Isaiah 31:4. We would understand that her picture of "lion" was associated with pain and damage. Unfortunately, many Christians are not very tolerant of anyone who finds God the Father a less-than-comforting picture. Since it is the most popular biblical image of God, too many assume that it is the *only* acceptable one.

God: More Than Father

In fact, however, survivors who wince at the word *father* do not have to give up prayer. Praying to Jesus seems much easier to many because he treated men, women, and children alike with respectful compassion. There are also other names and biblical images for God that can be precious alternatives when *father* is weighted with the pain of the past. The Psalmist addresses many prayers to God, "My Rock" (Ps. 18, 28, and so on). Other pictures of God from Scripture include the good shepherd (Luke 15:4–7; Ps. 23); the fortress (Ps. 18:2); the eagle (Deut. 32:11); the celebrating hostess (Luke 15:8–10); the woman in childbirth (Isa. 42:14–16); the mother of an infant (Ps. 131:2); the nursing mother (Isa. 47:14, 15); the lamb (Isa. 53:7); the mother bird (Ps. 91:4); the lion (Isa. 31:4); the king of glory (Ps. 24:7–10); and so forth. Why not explore prayers that use each of these and the many other biblical images? A brief prayer (or the reading of Ps. 31:1–5) while imagining the shelter and the warmth of a thick rock fortress can help build new, healthy images of divine protection and peace.

Taking time out from the overused Father God images is not valuable only to survivors of sexual abuse. It is a way for all of us to broaden our understanding of who God is. Concentrating on only one view of God creates a static unbiblical image—a finite, physical, limited picture of a Spirit who is infinite. This is a type of idolatry, worshiping a "graven image" rather than a biblical God. God is both male and female (and in God's image we are created male and female); both lion and lamb; both king of kings and suffering servant. All of these pictures offer perspectives that can illuminate the nature of God.[2]

For many women survivors who came from homes steeped in the hatred and abuse of women, the biblical pictures of God as a mother (Isa. 66:13, and so on) can give a special boost to self-esteem. Female images of God in Scripture remind us that femininity—as well as masculinity—is patterned upon this Infinite Creator.[3]

These verses also help many survivors who were hurt by their mothers to reframe that aspect of God as Parent. Two women told us that Isaiah 49:15 was especially precious to them because it pictures God as a nursing mother who will never abandon the suckling infant. Perhaps because Gerri's sexual abuse by her mother began while she was still hardly out of her babyhood and in the stage during which most children are most deeply attached to their mothers, she was still overwhelmed by it. Gerri quoted the Isaiah passage from memory. "I suppose I have a need for a Father," she told us, "but oh! I have always really *wanted* to have a Mother!"

Connie was not sexually abused by her mother, but the image of God-as-nursing-mother was meaningful for a different reason: "I call my mom a 'dry breast,'" she said with a rueful grin. "I just couldn't get any milk from her! She would routinely 'forget' to pick me up on time—and would show up for me two to four hours late. She sent me to school with thick knots in my hair. She abandoned me emotionally. I wanted a mother who combed my hair and picked me up on time. I wanted a mother who cared about me. This verse says that *God* will not forget me; God is a mother who will not abandon me."

Seeing Father in a Positive Light

Reframing God the Father is also a long-term goal of importance to survivors, although many need to wait months—or even years—before wrestling with the issue directly. Just as scriptural assurances help build a good concept of mother, well-loved passages like the parable of the prodigal son (Luke 15) help reframe the view of father.

Another vital step in this process is to create healthy relationships with other people. Having trusting, non-sexualized relationships with men (a pastor or a therapist for example[4]) can be very helpful. These relationships give new and more healthy pictures of the male and/or Father aspect of God.

Several women told us that watching their own husbands give love that was appropriate to their children helped heal their view of father. "I remember standing in the kitchen one day," Ruth said, "and my husband John poked his head in and whispered, 'Honey, come watch Tammy. She's trying to be sexy!' So I came out and there she was—at 4—wiggling around that living room in my high heels. She was fluttering her eyes at John and he was trying not to laugh.

"For a moment I was so afraid I started to shake. Then I looked at John, and I knew that she was safe with him. He said, 'Don't grow up too fast, Pumpkin.' Then he went back to his newspaper. I stood there and thought, 'So this is what fathers are supposed to be like.'"

Single women reported that just being around families where the fathers know how to balance protection and encouragement improved their view of God as Parent.

Acknowledging the Original Father

Even here, however, some caution must be exercised. Inevitably, even healthy parents make mistakes, sometimes serious ones. Remember that while life events can build or distort our image of God, *God is more than simply the projection of our own experiences.*

It is only human to take a look at the biblical pictures we have of God and relate them to our own experiences, but it is a falsely narrow frame. To assume God is just a bigger version of "father" or "shepherd" or "lamb" is rationally absurd—but that does not mean that it does not feel true, especially to someone who struggles with childhood trauma of any kind. "I think God is just like my father" is a comment consistently made in support groups for incest survivors. Inevitably, it is a comment made with fear or anger or despair. "If God is Father, and father is the abuser, then God must be the Super Abusive Parent."[5] It is only sensible to be wary of this God.

C. S. Lewis, grief-stricken over the death of his wife from cancer, expressed this dark terror eloquently: "My real fear is . . . that we are really rats in a trap. Or, worse still, rats in a laboratory. Someone said, I believe, 'God always geometrizes.' Supposing the truth were 'God always vivisects?' "[6] For children who have been deliberately hurt by those who are supposed to protect them, this ugly view of God will seem familiar. This is the mad scientist God who cannot be trusted.

But, as Lewis realized the next morning and recorded in his journal, this image is "too anthropomorphic" to fit God:

. . . . the picture [of God] I was building up last night is simply the picture of a man . . . who used to sit next to me at dinner and tell me what he'd been doing to the cats that afternoon. Now a being like [that man], however magnified, couldn't invent or create or govern anything. He would set traps and try to bait them. But he'd never have thoughts of baits like love, or laughter, or daffodils, or a frosty sunset. *He* make a universe? He couldn't make a joke, or a bow, or an apology, or a friend.[7]

The picture of God as Parent is always distorted if we take any human as the primary model for father (or mother, for that matter). If God is the Supreme Being, the Primary Life Force, the Alpha and Omega, then *God is the original model for parenting, not just the jumbo-sized imitation of some mortal man or woman.* In fact, St. Paul emphasizes this when he calls God "the Father . . . from whom all fatherhood in heaven and on earth derives its name" (Eph. 3:14).

And how are children to relate to this Parent? Just two sentences earlier, Paul insists "we may approach God with freedom and confidence" (Eph. 3:12).

Exploring the biblical prayers of chapter 6 and using all of the scriptural names for God are both approaches that can build "freedom and confidence" in God the Father. While such a change in feeling will not happen quickly, these approaches can give direct and comforting experience with the original model for fathering, a Parent with a "love that surpasses knowledge." This love surpasses even the knowledge and dark memories of pain, of injustice, and of evil.

Chapter 8

THE SURVIVOR AND EVIL

Gerri's hands shook slightly as she reached for another cigarette. "The memories of the occult rituals are worse than anything else," she said. "I remember several people chanting and caressing me. A tall man stood facing me, dressed in a black robe with a hood. He said, 'The demons Lust and Dominion will be within you and control you all of your life.' Then he raped me.

"I was only about 6 years old when this happened. I have never been able to see the faces of the people in that memory," Gerri said, quietly. "I can see their bodies and I can hear the man's voice but I can never see the faces. It may be because I have so much fear. . . ." her voice trailed off.

When the memory of this ceremonial rape as well as several other memories of sadistic sexual ritual returned to Gerri, her depression became intense. "My therapist, who was a former pastor, had been tremendously supportive as I worked through my memories of being prostituted by my father and molested by my mother. He really did not know what to do, however, with the ritual abuse scenes which emerged after I had been in therapy for several months. It was his belief that a Christian could not be possessed, yet I had become a Christian many years after the childhood experience and a decade before I came to see him. He *was* convinced that the ritual experiences had deeply scarred me spiritually, but he had no suggestions about how I could overcome the sense that the ceremony when I was six was still affecting my life.

Despite his assurances, I continued to *feel* possessed. Experiences you might call "paranormal" have always been a part of my life (knowing certain events ahead of time, etc.) but they began to increase and become frightening. Along with this, I regularly heard two voices telling me to commit suicide.

"I finally asked several friends to pray for my deliverance from these two demons. After they had prayed and laid hands upon me, I asked them to take turns staying with me and praying so that I would not be alone in the house and would not be tempted to kill myself."

The frenzied violence and noise often associated with a deliverance from demonic possession were not a part of Gerri's experience. "For me, the deliverance seemed to be a process. There was nothing scary going on; I made sure of that because my preschool daughters were both at home," she said. In fact, Gerri's description of the weekend session sounds closer to an intense prayer meeting than a scene from the *The Exorcist*. As the prayer vigil continued, Gerri reported that the oppressive sense of an evil presence lessened along with the "commands" to kill herself. "At 4:00 A.M., I heard the voices on the porch, telling me to let them in and to kill myself. Two hours later I heard them again—but this time, from the vacant lot across the street. Finally, the voices stopped."

Gerri's sense of deliverance was a tremendous relief. It was not, however, the end of all her emotional and spiritual reactions to the years of sexual abuse she had survived. She continued to pursue healing in every way she could: she remained in individual therapy on a two-to-four-times-a-week basis and continued on antidepressant medication. She required hospitalization for one six-week period. She stayed for several months in a group therapy situation and eventually joined a church-based support group for survivors. She also met weekly with two women who prayed with her for inner healing.

Satanic Overtones

Gerri's memories of an occult ritual combined with child rape are difficult to consider without revulsion. Gerri's parents had already involved her in prostitution and pornography, and they may have been willing to "rent" her body to some bizarre cult group (there are also some clues that one member of her family may have been involved in occult practice); but could a religious group using ritual forms of sexual abuse exist in modern America?

Reports from child interview conducted by therapists, police officers, and social workers have included descriptions of rituals similar to the one in Gerri's story. Sociologist David Finkelhor's recent study on sexual abuse in day-care settings identified "at least 36 substantiated sexual-abuse cases in which some ritualistic element was noted by investigators." He noted that "clear-cut corroboration of ritualistic practices was available in a few cases, such as Country Walk [Dade County, Florida], where ritual objects were found by police, and where the female perpetrator did admit to some of the sadistic practices alleged in the children's stories."[1] The National Child assault Prevention Project recently published the following definition of ritual abuse:

> Ritualistic does not necessarily mean satanic. "Ritualistic" merely means a "ceremonial act or customarily repeated act or series of acts." Many of the ritual abuse cases, however, do appear to have satanic overtones, and many cases reported in different parts of the country involve ritual acts that are almost identical in nature.[2]

While there have always been sex crimes which involve sadistic ritual, the official reports of religious or satanic practice as part of child abuse allegations are fairly recent. Some of these cases appear to be "pseudo-ritualistic abuse" where pedophiles were motivated by sexual attraction to children rather than religious conviction and used the trappings of the occult to scare children into cooperating. Certainly, bizarre fear-inducing ceremonies make children less likely to tell and even less likely to be believed. In other cases, the perpetrators abuse children ritualistically as part of their own obsessive or delusional psychopathology rather than cult-based religion.[3]

In at least some of the cases, however, "there appears to be a deliberate attempt at inculcation of ideology."[4] This ideology centers on a calculated attempt to convince the child that she is beyond the reach of God.

1. *God is good:* Satan or evil takes the place of God as the object of worship in ritual abuse and the spiritual goal is not righteousness but wickedness. The attack on a child's value system is overt. In many cases, children have reported that they are forced to do simple—slightly repugnant—tasks

(like poking the eyes out of a cartoon figure) to avoid being punished, but that the "next task is less simple and the next even less."[5] Eventually, the child must do something that violates her principles such as "killing (or thinking they were killing) animals or babies, torturing other children, or eating (or believing they were eating) pets, humans, feces, or urine."[6] The stigma of the sexual abuse and the shame of participating in such actions push the child toward identifying herself with evil rather than goodness. She feels irrevocably cut off from a good God.

2. *God is love:* In sadistic rituals, hurting victims is part of an act of worship to a dangerous devil-god. A Satan who hates and wishes to destroy is in stark contrast to the God who "so loved the world" before we felt any love and while we were yet sinners. To pray to Satan with the freedom of expression with which we can come before a loving God (as we explored in chapter 6) would be suicidal. Only unconditional love allows free expression of feeling. For the survivor of ritual abuse, any kind of relationship—including (or especially) a relationship with God—is fraught with danger.

3. *God is powerful:* Satan's power is the power of violence and hatred. The power of love is rejected. The cross—the symbol of suffering for the sake of others—is turned upside down in satanist practice. The power of individual choice is also diminished; indeed the most consistent aspect of all ritual abuse is the attack upon the victim's free will.[7] Jesus called his disciples friends, not servants (John

15:15), but in the world of abusive ritual, Satan has no friends, only slaves.

4. *God is parent:* While God is the creator of all life, Satan has been called the Father of Murder. The emphasis in sadistic ritual is not physical or emotional nurturance and life, but victimization, pain, or even death. Survivors describe rites which include the sacrifice of animals, the use of corpses, the symbols of death, or even the murder of living victims.

Finkelhor speculates that one motive for ritualistic abuse may be that adults who see their own sexuality as corrupted, evil or demonic may feel resentment or hatred toward the pure or uncorrupted sexuality of children. As a result, he suggests, they may harbor "an intense desire to harm, corrupt, retaliate against, or in our concept 'mortify' the sexuality of a small child because of its innocence."[8]

A Perspective on Recovery

The survivors of sadistic rituals have been traumatized in ways which make them feel like evil, powerless, and unloved sexual objects. Therapists who work with these survivors combine child sexual abuse treatment with what one described as "de-programming" methods to help reframe their distorted view of reality. For Christian survivors, special assistance may be needed to overcome the distortion of their faith.

In her recovery, Gerri used every support available to her to overcome the fear that she was beyond the reach of God. She memorized Romans 8:38: "For I am convinced that neither death nor life, neither angels nor demons . . . nor anything else in all creation, will be able to separate us from the love of God. . . ."

She discovered, however, that at her own church she was regarded with suspicion by two opposing groups. The ones who accepted the deliverance objected to her continued need for therapy, medication and support; those who understood the therapy were distressed by her positive experience with a spiritual deliverance. Even those who agreed that there was demonic involvement were divided about whether she was possessed or only "oppressed" by their presence.

Despite the controversy, we have included Gerri's story as a contribution to the ongoing discussion on ritual abuse and as an encouragement to others who identify with her experience—not as a definitive statement on the issues raised. We applaud her effort to arm herself with every tool in the recovery process. We were not present at the deliverance ceremony she described and are certainly not experts in demon possession or exorcism. It seems clear, however, that any ritual is a powerful way to act out and recognize an inner commitment and that there is a certain logic to using healing ritual to counterbalance the impact of sadistic rites. But Gerri's experience illustrates that even in those cases, spiritual deliverance serves only limited purposes and is not a quick cure for long-term issues.[9]

For some survivors who were not ritual abuse victims, such a ceremony has actually been counterproductive. Connie also participated in a deliverance. Entering the service, her expectations were high. However, the deliverance ceremony left her still plagued with the same nagging symptoms of suicidal depression. The sense that the deliverance had "failed" left Connie in a deeper despair and brought all recovery to a halt for weeks. "I was so angry that I wasn't cured," she said. "But my therapist and the group kept telling me, 'We're still here for you.' Finally, I realized that demons weren't the problem—I had been trying to circumvent the process."

The inner voices that many survivors hear (and this symptom is common) usually belong to the significant people in their past. The experience of sexual invasion, however, makes some victims especially vulnerable to the idea that they are possessed even if there is no evidence of occult involvement or ritual abuse. "I was penetrated by something evil," the survivor feels—and wrongly assumes that this sense is proof of a satanic attack.[10] This belief is particularly terrifying if she feels that she is isolated from God and powerless against such a force. The truth, however, is that evil has deep limits to its power. The biblical Satan, after all, is a fallen creation, not the creator. Survivors of all types of abuse—including ritual abuse—should avoid giving the Devil more than his due. As Romans 8:39 makes clear, even the rulers of hell cannot separate someone from the love of God.

It is fascinating to note that in the story of Job, the opening chapters show Satan asking God's permission to afflict a good man. The permission is given—but only within God-given boundaries. And, while Satan strives to cast himself as the prime mover in Job's tribulation, he is actually given only a cameo role with no speaking part in the forty-two chapter narrative after the second chapter. Instead, Job's three "friends" become the spiritual adversaries as they present theological reasons for his suffering; reasons that both God and Job ultimately reject. The drama revolves around Job and his God—their impassioned speeches, their honesty, and their relationship. Job realizes God is the only one with the power to bring about justice and restoration and tirelessly presents his case to the Almighty. He doesn't waste words on Satan.

Keeping this biblical example in mind is particularly useful since blaming the Devil can be a convenient way to escape personal responsibility. One support group had a member who opened her comments during a session with the assertion, "Satan told me not to come tonight, but I came anyway." The group leader responded by asking, "Jane, is there a part of you that does not want to be here and resists coming to group?" Jane denied any personal conflict about coming but throughout the evening continued to make reference to the things she claimed Satan had told her directly. The level of tension in the group began to grow.

Normally reluctant to stop any kind of sharing, the group leader decided that this was destructive. "We are here tonight to talk about ourselves and our feelings. I am going to ask that we not talk about Satan because that shifts our focus. Questions about Satan's power can be discussed with your therapist or with your pastor or priest, but they are counterproductive in group. Let's remember that not even the powers of hell can prevail against the love of God."

Two group members were unhappy with the decision, but several other women approached the leader later to admit that they had been badly frightened. The enforcement of this kind of a boundary on the discussion made them feel that the group would continue to be a safe place—not a fearful place. It also ended Jane's attempts to indoctrinate others with her religious views, and she began to talk in a more honest and self-revealing way.

The Illusion of Safety

In some ways, it would be easier to accept if child abuse was something that *only* happened within satanist cult groups. In fact, these reports are present in only a tiny minority of the hundreds of thousands of child sexual abuse cases. Child molesters are far more likely to be members of a local church than a devil worshipping cult. Pedophiles have no particular "look;" they can be any age and either gender. Many perpetrators are described by their friends and families as being kind and helpful. It is not unusual for them to be active and committed members or even on the professional staff of church and para-church groups.

"My father was an evil man," Sharon said firmly. "So I thought that if I could just avoid men like my father, I would be okay." She paused and shrugged. "It hasn't turned out to be quite that simple.

"My first husband—who was a youth minister—left me after several affairs. I was in serious financial and emotional trouble and I began therapy with James, a highly regarded counselor. The sessions meant so much to me. He really helped me work through my feelings about men.

"James even helped me find a teaching job and encouraged me to finish my master's degree. He and his wife had me over for dinner. I started attending their church. When my son—who was then 12—seemed depressed over the divorce, James offered to counsel him. I was delighted; James is a specialist in adolescent psychology! Timmy agreed to see him. I never asked Tim how the sessions went; I really regarded the therapist-client relationship as sacred. After several weeks, Tim came up with some excuse to stop his sessions with James, but I continued my own therapy sessions for many months. When I was ready to deal with my childhood memories of abuse, however, I switched to a woman counselor who specialized in incest recovery.

"For the next ten years, James and his wife Marge were my best friends. They attended my wedding to my second husband. They watched my children grow up. Then last year, James was arrested for child molestation. Hundreds of photographs of children in sexual acts were discovered, including videotapes in which James appears. The most terrifying revelation, however, was that Tim had been one of his victims."

Months of dealing with the deep sense of betrayal followed. "I lost all confidence in my own instincts," she said. "Why didn't I know this about James?" Later, however, she realized there had been some clues she had chosen to ignore, including James's deeply troubled relationship with his own son. Sharon also remembered two dinner conversations where James had defended child-adult sexual relationships as "psychologically healthy." While he had said glibly it was a "purely academic" matter of interest, Sharon was distressed by his comments.

Courtesy, gratitude, and a reluctance to believe that a man who could demonstrate such good qualities was capable of hurting a child kept Sharon from pursuing any of these questions with James. She even felt a bit guilty about harboring any suspicions. "After all," she reasoned, "he is so different from my father!"

Many weeks after the discovery about James, Sharon enrolled in a clay modeling seminar. The emphasis was on self-expression rather than art, and she immediately became intent on working with the pliable material in her hands. First, she formed two matching angel wings reaching up around a small head in an arc, the body curving down toward the base. Impulsively, she took a small piece of clay and modeled it into a swaddled infant to place in the angel's arms. Just as she began to add the baby to the sculpture, however, she started back in alarm. The wings were too close to the head. The sculpture did not look like an angel at all; it was the sinewy body and massive "winged" head of a deadly cobra.

"It was James," she explained, her eyes filling with tears. "I thought he was an angel, but he was a viper. And I gave him my baby!"

Betrayal of Innocence

The reality of child sexual abuse destroys the assumption that life is fair or that the world is a benign and safe place. Nothing is a more compelling argument for the existence of evil than the betrayal of innocence. Ever since Eden, men and women have been given the freedom to choose between good and evil, and when they make evil choices, others—including innocent children—are inevitably affected.

This is, of course, a very limited answer to the question of why the innocent suffer. While there are many fine theological books on this topic, it is interesting to note that Job himself got few details on this pressing and painful issue. God listened carefully to Job's complaints, praised him, and ultimately reinstated his good fortune. But to the critical question of "Why?" God's only response was that Job was not God.

Novelist Frederich Buechner speculates:

Maybe the reason God doesn't explain to Job why terrible things happen is that he knows what Job needs isn't an explanation. Suppose that God did explain . . . And then what? Understanding in terms of the divine economy why his children had to die. Job would still have to face their empty chairs at breakfast every morning. Carrying in his pocket straight from the horse's mouth a complete theological justification of his boils, he would still have to scratch and burn.[11]

All explanations of evil and suffering—however compelling—leave us to "scratch and burn." But suffering as an experience can be shared and it is often in sharing our pain that healing occurs. Such sharing, after all, is the purpose of the Incarnation and the true mission of the Church. The stigma which is attached to sexual abuse victims, however, can cut them off from a loving God, supportive communities, and the healing process. Such isolation has been described as the 'breeding ground of evil' and it can put a child at spiritual risk for continuing the victim-perpetrator cycle.

Two ways in which the evil of child abuse is repeated through successive generations of children include:

1. *Evil and Pathology: The Re-Enactment of Trauma.* While child molestation is evil, most molestors do not fit the profile of "evil" people. Typically, perpetrators use children to re-enact uncon-

sciously the trauma of their own childhood and are as caught in their own pathology as their victims. In one case, a sex offender actually arranged his living room furniture to match the room in which he had been molested as a boy, a fact he consciously suppressed until several months into therapy! Many perpetrators, of course, were not molested as children, but it is safe to say that all were hurt in some significant way during their own childhood.

The repetition of trauma works with grim efficiency. Children who get hurt often grow up to hurt children. Even a perpetrator's compulsive sexual attraction to children, however, reveals an internal push toward being confronted by the deepest internal wound. But, the longer offenders blindly reenact their pain, the less likely they are to really face, deal with or recover from the original damage. Until they do that, they are unlikely to take responsibility for the pain they cause. Instead, child molestors often convince themselves that the sexual relationship is helping the child and that their victims (even if the perpetrator is involved with dozens of children simultaneously) are truly in love with them.

2. *Evil and Personality: People of the Lie.* A personality disorder Peck describes as "evil" is the most extreme form of this abrogation of responsibility typical of perpetrators. He notes the following distinguishing characteristics:
   (a) consistent destructive, scapegoating behavior, which may often be quite subtle.

(b) excessive, albeit usually covert, intolerance to criticism and other forms of narcissistic injury.

(c) pronounced concern with a public image and self-image of respectability, contributing to a stability of life-style but also to pretentiousness and denial of hateful feelings or vengeful motives.

(d) intellectual deviousness, with an increased likelihood of a mild schizophreniclike disturbance of thinking at times of stress.[12]

Looking at the list, Sharon said, "Yes, that describes my father, doesn't it? In all my growing up years, I never heard him take responsibility for anything wrong; yet he caused so much pain." Sharon's honesty may shock some, but it is a tribute to her health. Peck notes, "It is doubtful that some can be wholly healed of their scars from having had to live in close quarters with evil without correctly naming the source of their problems."[13]

In today's world it is unpopular to talk about sin or evil acts or evil people. Yet, Christ had few anxieties about holding those who hurt children responsible for their actions. Understanding that innocent victims of sexual abuse are at spiritual risk of becoming lifelong victims or perpetrators themselves brings fresh understanding to these passionate words of Jesus:

. . .whoever welcomes a little child like this in my name welcomes me. But if anyone causes one of these little ones who believe in me to sin, it would be better for him to have a large millstone hung around his neck and to be drowned in the depths of the sea. . . . If your hand or your foot causes you to sin, cut it off and throw it away. It is better for you to enter life maimed or crippled than to have two hands or two feet and be thrown into eternal fire. . . .

See that you do not look down on one of these little ones. For I tell you that their angels in heaven always see the face of my Father in heaven" (Matt. 18:5, 6, 8, 10).

The word Jesus used for "causes . . . to sin" carries the meaning "entice" or "entrap." It is particularly apt phrasing for child sexual abuse. No one reading this passage could doubt Jesus' anger at any action that damages children. It is also clear that Christ holds the adult—not the child—responsible for such sin.

But what are we to make of the violent suggestions to that adult? If everyone with a sin problem took this literally, few Christians would keep all their body parts! It is doubtful that Jesus had any intention of encouraging people to actually amputate limbs. He chose, however, the most powerful language possible to insist that responsibility be taken. People resist painful change. Yet Christ insists that the adult who hurts a child bear any pain and suffer any loss in order to change that pattern.

While Jesus' words are stern, there is as much hope here for the perpetrator as for the victim. Jesus makes it clear that if decisive action is taken, change *can* happen and moral disaster can be averted. Recovery from this sexual addiction is possible but it is not easy and it takes a type of spiritual amputation.

An excellent example of the directive support perpetrators need in order to make this change is found in an essay by Marie Fortune entitled, "Forgiveness, The Last Step":

One incest offender approached his pastor and told him that he had been molesting his daughter for two years: Could God forgive him and could the pastor forgive him? The pastor assured him that God forgives those who repent of their sin, and then he offered to pray with him. He also said that as soon as they were finished praying, he (the pastor) wanted the father to call the Child Protection Service and report himself. The man was surprised; but he did as he was instructed. Then the pastor explained to the man that he would eventually be placed in a treatment program for incest offenders and the pastor wanted him to attend that program once a week. He also wanted to see him once a week for Bible study and prayer and he wanted him in church every Sunday.

The pastor could easily have said a prayer over this man and sent him home. The offender would have felt absolved of any responsibility and, although genuinely desiring at that moment not to repeat the offense, would be highly likely to do so. Instead, the minister used the authority of his pastoral office to give guidance and direction to the offender, which he knew would be in the offender's best interest in the long run.[14]

The only way out of the trap is to go back to the pain and move through it with the love, support, and restraints of a community. (See the chart in Chapter 2.)

It is in this opportunity for change and redemption that God's ultimate answer to evil lies. God also had an innocent child betrayed. The Christian viewpoint, however, is that the betrayal and death of Jesus was the beginning of the end for evil. The Christian God did not triumph over evil by destroying it, but by absorbing it ("He became sin for us") and transforming victimization into resurrection. It is in this great metaphor that every survivor—indeed every perpetrator—can find hope and new life.

Chapter 9

THE SURVIVOR AND FORGIVENESS

"It was easy for me to forgive my brother-in-law at first," Kate admitted during a group session, "because basically, I still blamed myself for the incest." Because children are egocentric, they are especially vulnerable to the idea that they cause everything. Children often feel guilt over their parents' divorce, a grandparent's death, or a sibling's life-threatening disease. The same phenomenon occurs in child sexual abuse: the child herself feels guilty. Thus, the same child who sees herself as worthless and shameful and "skinless" can in the next moment be convinced that she somehow "caused" the abuse and could have stopped it. Letting go of that false sense of power and accepting that as children they could not really have controlled a sexual relationship with an adult is tremendously difficult for survivors. The developmental task of building a realistic sense of what power she has and what her human boundaries are has never been completed.

It is for this reason that the area of forgiveness must be approached with sensitivity and caution. Most incest victims have survived a dysfunctional family system by denying what they really feel, taking responsibility for the actions of others, and pretending that everything is just fine. Therefore, many of them will rush through the same coping pattern as adults, adding a sugarcoated spirituality to the recipe. This is not forgiveness, and certainly, it does not lead to healing or wholeness. Survivors have to recognize that they have been wronged before they can forgive.

"In my healing process," Connie noted, "it was critical for me to finally blame my family for the abuse. I had to finally admit, 'Look, they did *not* do the best they could.' They were *wrong. Nobody* should be treated like that!"

"I think before you forgive," Donna added thoughtfully, "you have to try and get the facts straight. For me, it took a process of finding out where all this suicidal depression came from, and that meant looking at how I had been hurt as a child and at the people who had caused me the pain. At first, I wanted to forgive everybody before I figured out what they had done and why and how it damaged me. Staying with those feelings until memories came back was tough. It did not feel Christian because I always thought God wanted you to have only good feelings toward other people, and looking at my pain made all those feelings of rage and betrayal come back.

"Mostly, my Christian friends had a hard time thinking it was okay for me to focus on blame at all. They did not see any point in exploring the losses I had suffered. They just wanted me to 'forgive and forget.'"

David Augsburger has written, "When forgiveness denies that there is anger, acts as if it never happened, smiles as though it never hurts, fakes as though it is all forgotten . . . it is not forgiveness. It's a magical fantasy."[1]

It is very instructive to reflect on how Jesus really dealt

with the religious and civil leaders who attacked him. It is true that Jesus urged his followers to "love your enemies and pray for those who persecute you," (Matt. 5:44), and that he asked God to forgive his enemies even as he died. But we must not ignore the complexity of his response to those who were trying to hurt him. He did not pretend that they had never wronged him and that they were all one happy family. In fact, he took every opportunity to confront them on their opposition to him. He did not say nice things about them nor protect their well-established reputations. He accused them of the sin of hypocrisy and called them "vipers" (Matt. 23:33) and "sons of hell" (Matt. 23:15).

He did not trust his enemies and he accurately predicted that they would eventually murder him (Matt. 16:21: Luke 9:22) and persecute his followers (Matt. 23:34–35). He affirmed that God was in control of his ministry and even his death, but noted that those who betrayed him bore a terrible responsibility for their actions (Luke 11:50; Matt. 23:35–36). Consistently, Jesus recognized and met his own needs in a healthy way. The night before he died, he admitted that the actions of Judas and his enemies had caused him intense suffering and he actively sought the support of his friends in facing the pain.

Christlike forgiveness is based on a total commitment to telling the truth. While the biblical model opposes seeking personal vengeance, it does not exclude the expression of anger or even some appropriate name-calling. True forgiveness is not at odds with pointing out clearly who bears the responsibility for a sin.

People who confuse "fantasy forgiveness" with Christlike forgiveness assume that a person who tells the truth, admits her pain, grieves her losses, and expresses her feelings is involved only in the process of anger or even hatred. They assume that anger is proof of the absence of love. The truth is that love and anger are linked from the moment of our births.

The Love Cycle

Learning to love is the very first order of business for the human infant. The process is not only difficult and time-consuming, but also involves feelings that are unpleasant and frightening. Magid and McKelvey trace the human bonding or love cycle through the following stages: (1) need, (2) rage reaction, (3) gratification or relief, and (4) trust.[2] The infant feels a painful awareness of need—hunger or cold or loneliness—and instinctively responds to this potentially life-threatening need with a "rage reaction." Even if the child's physical needs are met, her emotional needs to be held and loved must also be relieved consistently for the infant to learn to love.

Neglected infants who are not held or nurtured eventually give up their angry cries and settle into an eerie and silent wait for death. These babies who "fail to thrive" are the most extreme examples of what happens when the child's environment is rejecting. Many children receive enough attention to live but not enough to bond to another person. These are the adults who are at risk of never developing the ability to trust or love.

The "bonding cycle" illustrates how limited our view of love and trust and, ultimately, forgiveness is. Child development specialists tell us that babies need to feel and express their discomfort and bad feelings and get a kind and fairly predictable response from their parents in order to achieve trust, and eventually, love.

Parents who rush to meet the child's every need before she feels and communicates her distress are not necessarily being helpful; anger is part of the learning process. Once the child realizes that she has "good-enough"[3] parents who respond to her needs and hold her even though she has bad and frightening feelings, she begins the process of trust. This "holding environment" is required to support a child through hundreds or even thousands of trips around the cycle of need-rage-relief-trust. It is this bond—based on the expression of need—that is the foundation for love.

Parents who neglect or abuse the needy child traumatically interrupt the love cycle. If a child was ignored—or even punished—when she expressed pain, acknowledging her own neediness can be terrifying and dangerous.

A story that Kate told the group illustrates the effects of this kind of neglect or abuse. "You know, my mom used to have a dog that we called Sidewinder because it would walk bent almost in half," she remembered. "This dog managed to walk forward and look backward at the same time! I kept thinking about that dog for years, knowing it was a significant picture for a long time before I realized the connection. Then I remembered that Sidewinder's walk was perfectly normal when my mother got him as a puppy. That crazy walk was *learned behavior*. She used to smack him with no warning at all, and he knew you couldn't turn your back on her."

Safe Places for Completing the Cycle

Pushing survivors into "fantasy forgiveness" can mean putting them right back into the dangerous, dysfunctional world their inner child knows so well. Kate explained, "My mother was completely unsupportive when I told her about my experience with my uncle—the same man who had molested her. Of course, as far as my experience with my brother-in-law went, she was very clear all along that I was the guilty party. Since I had harbored so much anger at her for her neglect of me over the years, however, I felt I needed to forgive her. Also, my Christian friends were pressuring me to contact her. So one day a few months ago, I phoned her up and said, 'Mom, I still hurt a lot because of the way you treated me when I was growing up. I want you to know, though, that I forgive you for hurting me and I want a relationship with you now.'

"Well, there was this long pause and then she started screaming. She told me—at the top of her lungs—'You deserved everything you got! You were a rotten little self-centered slut!' Then she hung up.

"I shook for the next two hours. I felt as if she had taken my heart, twisted it, and thrown it back at me. I kept saying, 'She's doing it to me AGAIN.'"

Kate's experience vividly illustrates how vulnerable adult survivors of childhood trauma are to being re-abused. Telling the truth to the same dysfunctional family—even after years have passed—can trigger the same denial and rejection (or silence and disbelief) that have kept the Inner Child isolated and split from herself. An adult facing this response from her family is likely to be emotionally thrown back to precisely the same inner rejection she felt as a child. It is good to work toward forgiveness and love, but it is very unusual for survivors to return to the same repressive and/or abusive family system and be allowed to freely express their emotions and achieve acceptance and love.

No one wants to get stuck in the infant "rage reaction" forever. Love is the goal, and the ability to forgive is eventually part of that package. Anyone who is recovering from child sexual abuse needs to find safe places to complete the developmental tasks ahead. A dysfunctional family is not the place to start, no matter how much the idea of forgiveness and reconciliation may appeal to the survivor. Instead, the skill of expressing feelings can be practiced (1) with a therapist, (2) with a support group, and (3) through your own "inner work" or spiritual journey (prayers, journaling, etc.). We strongly recommend that survivors pursue all three of these avenues for healing simultaneously during at least the first twelve to twenty-four months of recovery (more information on implementing this model is included in "Suggestions for Survivors" and "Shopping for Help" in the Appendix).

By building relationships in these safe places, survivors can begin the individuation process from their families. Once they can practice loving and being loved in a healthy way, survivors are far better equipped to approach the issue of forgiveness with realistic expectations.

Keeping Expectations Realistic

A dangerous aspect of "fantasy forgiveness" is that it inflames false expectations that can keep the survivor locked into dysfunctional relationships. It is important to remember that forgiveness may not include ever genuinely liking, enjoying, or having warm feelings toward a person who has harmed you; and may not include a reconciled relationship.

Some survivors report that after fully expressing their negative feelings about someone and exploring painful memories they are able to also appreciate positive aspects of the relationship. This is not, however, inevitable and if it does not happen, a survivor should not try to force herself to have warm feelings toward a person who has irreparably harmed her. There may, in fact, be very little to feel good about. That is not the basis or goal of forgiveness.

Reconciliation is also not the goal of forgiveness. Reconciliation requires agreement that a wrong has occurred and a mutual commitment to a healthy and safe relationship. Jesus forgave his enemies but did not have dinner with them after the Resurrection. They were not safe people and he did not trust them. *Even in his forgiveness, he kept his expectations realistic.*

The difficulty for incest survivors is that their most dangerous enemies are family members. Certainly, the ideal is for family members to love each other and remain in relationship. That is not something, however, that some disturbed families may be able to attain, no matter how earnestly the survivor herself may desire it.

As the group discussed the problem of reconciliation, Ruth said quietly, "It has been two years since I gave up on my parents. For years, John had asked me, 'Why do you spend so much time with these people? They don't act like they love you or even like you.' But I was sure it was the Christian thing to do. The last summer we went up to their place, however, my brother's oldest son George started following my daughter around. Sandy was only in fifth grade at the time and George was a junior in college. She found him peeking in her bedroom and bathroom windows, and he kept asking her to come with him on errands—invitations he didn't extend to the other children. When they were together, he would tell her dirty jokes. Sandy finally came to me and complained that he made her feel 'yucky.' I talked to my brother and sister-in-law who angrily insisted that Sandy was making a big deal out of nothing.

"For the next two days, Sandy and I were treated like pariahs. Sandy was devastated and convinced she had done something wrong. Finally, I confronted my parents over their lack of support or concern. George is a real favorite of my mother's (he actually lives with my parents because their home is close to his college) and she insisted there was no problem to discuss. 'You know how boys are,' she told Sandy sternly. My father—who has become more religious over the last few years—said piously that he would 'pray about it.'

"The next year, before we took our vacation, I called Dad and asked him if he had prayed about the situation. He said. 'Well, I've watched George with other little girls and I don't think he has a problem. Sandy should just keep out of his way this summer.'

"That did it. It was Uncle Fred all over again. They wanted my child to take responsibility and to control a man almost twice her age. I said, 'You have decided again to do nothing about a child in danger, so there can be no relationship. We won't be visiting your home. You are not safe people.' I had struggled again and again with the command to honor my parents but I knew I could not allow my children to be at risk. It is no coincidence that both Uncle Fred and George used my parents' house as home base. With my parents in charge, its open season on kids. Once I understood that, I gave up the dream that my family would somehow turn into the Waltons."

Even when reconciliation is achieved, the Inner Child's dream of a perfect relationship must be given up. "My mother has made a lot of changes," Connie noted. "For the first year of my recovery I simply could not contact her. Later, I would see her for brief visits— maybe a couple of hours. Now, she has met with me and my therapist three times over a period of several months.

"I had carried intense hatred of her for her neglect and lack of protection. Forgiving her was a process—not a onetime event—and while it took time, I can honestly say I have no desire for her to be punished for what she did. I have forgiven her. Letting go of my expectations of her was a big part of this. Even though she has come out of her denial about the sexual abuse, for example, she still can't really respond to me or my needs. I have had to realize that she has very limited resources emotionally. Now that I am an adult, however, I can get that nurturing from other, healthier people."

A forgiveness that allows for this awareness of another person's limits and emotional growth requires time and information. Beware of projecting what you need onto what the person who hurts you can give. Study what happened in the past to get a sense of what you might realistically expect in the future.

Forgive Them for They Know Not What They Do

It is helpful to remember that Jesus did not forgive his enemies because they did not "know better." Of course they knew better. They had intentionally conspired to send an innocent man to his death, and Jesus had confronted them with their responsibility and sin on several occasions. Instead, his prayer was, "Father, forgive them for they know not *what* they do" (Luke 23:34 KJV). His enemies had willfully shut their eyes to who he was and had not understood the scope of their sin. They thought they were permanently silencing a heretical rabbi who had criticized them; they certainly did not believe that they were murdering the Messiah.

In the same way, most sexual abuse perpetrators are ignorant of the scope of the damage they are inflicting. Sexually addicted, they cannot really see the victim for who she is or recognize the terrible impact of molestation. Usually this pattern of denial was entrenched in the abuser's own family of origin.

"It has been tremendously helpful for me to discover the unconscious patterns in my family," Connie told the group. "When I considered the sexual abuse my father endured from his mother; when I learned about the neglect of my own mother; when I traced alcoholism and abandonment through the family tree, it was as if a light went on. It did not excuse my parents. They still could have done a lot better by their children. But they refused to look at their lives, at what really occurred, and so they went on in lockstep with these destructive patterns."

Constructing a family tree or a genogram can be a

powerful tool to promote this type of insight into family members.[4] Many people discover that patterns emerge when they attach notes to the names on the family tree, indicating who abused alcohol or drugs, who was an abused child or a wife beater, who was raped, who committed suicide, and so on. These are the family secrets, ghosts that can haunt a family for years if they are not faced and acknowledged.

Tracing the family truth does not make it less painful, and as Connie pointed out, it does not justify abusive behavior. In fact, it reinforces the need for careful boundaries in dealing with perpetrators. A genogram's strength, however, is that it makes visible the fact that people who are blind to their own pain inevitably pass it down for generations. That perspective gives survivors a window to begin the process of understanding and forgiveness.

The genogram also illuminates the survivor's own potential blind spots. Many survivors resist the concept of a forgiveness that begins with blame because they take the verse, "Judge not that ye be not judged" out of context. In Matthew 7:1–5, however, Jesus does not forbid appropriate judgments; he provides guidelines on how to judge. He insists that in judging the actions of others we must also deal with the painful truths about ourselves—the "beam" in our own eye.

"When I looked at my family genogram," Ruth said, "I saw for the first time how many secrets were in our family closet. I could see the old family pain Sandy faces, and not just because of what George did, either. My harsh words, the times I've hit her in anger, are all part of the package. I decided I would not stay trapped like my parents. I refused to close my eyes to the evil

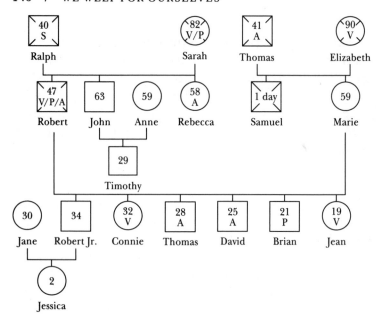

A = Alcoholic
S = Suicide
V = Victim of Sexual Abuse
P = Perpetrator of Sexual Abuse
Crossed Out Circle or Square = Deceased

Figure 4. Connie's Genogram

they did to me and," she paused and looked down, "the evil I've done to my children. I knew that only by the grace of God could we break this cycle. I just held that genogram and prayed, 'Oh, God, forgive me—forgive us all.'"

Chapter 10

THE SURVIVOR AND
WHOLENESS

Seeing how connected we all are to a human family system that passes along dysfunction and pain not only helps us to forgive those who have wronged us—it also helps us to forgive and accept the darkest and most shamed parts of ourselves. This helpful insight, however, is not enough by itself. Such acceptance must be experienced before we can practice it. Humans are social beings and as psychiatrist Irving Yalom has said emphatically, "It is the *relationship* that heals."[1]

It is this relational power to break through isolation which makes support groups such an effective tool of recovery. "A few weeks ago," Donna said, "I was so overwhelmed by feelings, memories, and fears that I could barely force myself to walk in the door. The session before, I had told you all about being molested by my dad, my anxiety about my own sexuality, everything. When I got to group the next time, I was so terrified I could not talk. I ended the evening curled up in a corner, sobbing. All of a sudden, I looked up and Connie was sitting next to me on the floor, with tears in her eyes. At the end of the meeting, everyone came up and hugged me. No one tried to fix me, no one tried to give me a Christian thought for the day. I had shared everything I was most ashamed of, but I have never felt so accepted.

"That was the most amazing experience," Donna said. "This group can actually listen to me share my bad feelings or cry and not reject me. Outside of therapy, I have never experienced that.

"I struggled with terrible depression when I was in fifth and sixth grade," Donna told the group. "My teacher sent a note home about my withdrawn behavior but I can't remember my parents ever asking me about that. I spent a lot of time alone. At home, I felt invisible. As long as I practiced piano and did my homework, no one seemed to notice my sadness.

"When I tried to tell my mother how lonely I was, she would observe that as a child she 'wasn't very popular either' (which was not the point) or deny that I really had a problem. Most of all, I remember thinking that she wanted me to leave her alone. Certainly she did not want to sit and hold me and feel my sorrow with me.

"Because our family was very religious and attended church several times a week, I began to talk about my depression in spiritualized terms. I was afraid I was not really 'saved.' Both of my parents told me to have more 'faith.'

"For a brief time after that, I tried going up the aisle and accepting Christ after every sermon. My embarrassed parents finally told me to stop that. It was very clear to me by then that God would have no more interest in or patience with my suffering than my parents had. Just as they could not hear a little girl asking, 'Do you love me even when I'm sad?' I could not believe that God would listen. He would be impatient.

He would tell me to do my homework and not to be so silly.

"So, for years I believed in that dysfunctional God. Not only that, I have internalized that God. Whenever I grow depressed for more than an 'acceptable' period, I become impatient and angry with my own suffering. The acceptable period of sorrow I allow myself seems to be about three minutes—which is about the amount of sustained attention I usually received from my parents."

Isolated from God and others, Donna locked up her sadness within, determined to believe in her parents' "perfect family" facade by rejecting her own experience and feelings. "When we are too fragile to bear guilt or profound grief," Kaplan has noted, ".... splitting takes over completely."[2]

We human beings are all too fragile to bear grief alone, which is why grieving as a community is so important.

Not every group, however, can provide an environment for mutually shared grief. Many church and parachurch groups, for example, unconsciously reinforce the denial and repression of feelings modeled by the unhealthy family.

"The administration of the campus ministry group that I worked for generally downplayed the importance of feelings," Connie remembered. "The teaching materials we used referred to the 'train' of life. We called the facts of God's word the 'engine;' our faith the 'coal car;' and our feelings the 'caboose.' In other words, you can't run the train with the caboose or let your feelings run your life. That makes sense, but you know," she said drolly, "if the caboose is sending up smoke and it is next to the coal car, you better stop and pay attention to it or that whole train is going to explode!"

While it is certainly true that most incest survivors received negative beliefs, a bankrupt theology, and a skewed understanding of what to expect in the world, the first wound they suffered was not cognitive but social and experiential: they were treated without love or respect. Those experiences led to splitting and arrested emotional development. For that reason, the most direct route to recovery is also social and experiential— support from a community that provides the healthy experience and development that was missed.

Groups that focus primarily on teaching can provide important information about child abuse, self-esteem, or the nature of God, but they are not the most effective approaches for emotional healing or developmental tasks. While there are good reasons for a didactic approach in many—perhaps most—church programs, setting up a support group for incest survivors on a Bible study or Sunday School model has inherent disadvantages. Too often, the survivor of a dysfunctional family responds to this approach by continuing the same codependent emotional patterns she learned as a child. She nods agreement to the doctrine ("God loves us" or "We must forgive our enemies") and suppresses her real feelings, her real experiences with God and others to comply with what she is being told. She may end up feeling more isolated and ashamed of her Inner Child than ever before. While she may find this same approach extremely helpful for learning facts about scripture and the Christian faith, she is not likely to attempt the primary tasks of recognizing her pain and connecting with others in this type of "classroom" setting.

Isolated by shame, she needs to learn love in the same way every baby must—by recognizing her distress and reaching out to others. This takes great persistence and humility. It takes a willingness to do what Jesus suggested, to spiritually become "a little child."

This experiential process cannot be bypassed by sophisticated and sincere beliefs about theology or psychology. This is not to imply that the survivor does not need new cognitive information about child abuse, self-esteem, and even the nature of God; this can be very helpful. She is far more likely to reframe her dysfunctional beliefs, however, once she has actually experienced mutual support and trust within a loving community.

It is for this reason that the central focus of an effective support group must be on creating an environment where each member is accepted regardless of her feelings or experiences. In such a group, it is safe to express feelings of great shame or rage or despair.

There is a biblical tradition for this kind of community grieving process, and it is overdue for rediscovery by the Church. In ancient times, God told Jeremiah to call for women "skillful" in mourning (Jer. 9:17) to lead Israel in grieving for its national losses. Bible scholar Dr. Renita Weems has suggested that Jeremiah himself may have been the son of a professional woman mourner[3]—a forerunner of Mary of Bethany. Certainly, this "weeping prophet" displayed an uncommon freedom to confront loss with emotional honesty. Women and men with the mourning skills of a Jeremiah or Mary have never been more needed than they are today.

It is interesting that Jesus himself spoke to this need for mourning up until the moment of his death. Indeed, the last "sermon" that Jesus preached before being nailed to the cross was addressed to the grieving women who gathered by the side of the road. His words indicate that Mary's jar of perfume and his night in Gethsemane had been effective; his own grief work was finally complete. "O Daughters of Jerusalem, do not weep for me," he told them. "Weep for yourselves and for your children . . . for if men do these things when the tree is green, what will happen when it is dry?" (Luke 23:28, 31).

Jesus' prediction of the future suffering of children (and the pain of those who love their children) is not a popular text for Sunday morning sermons. That is not hard to understand, for it is a disturbing passage. It describes future times filled with the suffering of women and children. The prophecy expresses the pain and frustration of anyone who has loved children and watched them suffer. The verses describe the sense of powerlessness felt by victims of all sorts of horrors: wars, enslavement, famine, and certainly, sexual assault. This agonized sermon undermines the hope that faith is a talisman to ward off difficulty, and instead presents tears as tools to help us face the inevitable injustices of life. Western Christians, however, have too often ignored our Lord's commandment to weep for ourselves and our children.

Building a Community

Building a community that can surround people who are in pain is a task much like building a family. It is complex and important and seldom has a day-to-day agenda. The primary focus must be on creating the nurturing environment that will allow group members to recognize and reveal the youngest, most vulnerable and damaged parts of themselves in safety. This requires a gentle, open approach rather than a tightly structured program that encourages members to stay in their "adult," cognitive, and/or competent selves.

Resistance to this approach, however, should be expected. Many people's initial reaction to community process is anxiety. They want order. They want organization. They want answers—from an authoritative leader. Facing uncomfortable feelings is not pleasant, which is why "splitting" is a tempting alternative.[4]

Donna admitted, "I have to tell you that at first, the support meetings really bothered me. I wanted the time to be more structured and I wanted answers—real answers—about why this had happened to me. I wanted to get some kind of spiritual 'reason' for what I went through. I really felt that our group was not getting the kind of leadership we needed. About the third week, when we were going around and telling our stories, I found myself getting more and more upset. 'What good does it do to keep talking about this?' I wondered.

"But by the end of the session, after I had told the group what had happened to me in my family bathroom, so many years ago, I looked around the room and realized that I was not alone. All my life the 4-year-old within me had been alone with that secret. Now she wasn't. I don't know why I felt so much relief, but I did."

Learning how to tolerate uncomfortable feelings and how to share them with a loving community is a vital part of mental health for everyone, not just survivors. Too often, people who have come from dysfunctional homes, however, have an unrealistic view of what health is. They cling to the view that if they can just find the key, they will become perfect, cured of their distressing emotions and problems, Ironically, this keeps them locked into the same perfectionistic, self destructive patterns. Kaplan calls the following four abilities, "constancy," the mark of real health and wholeness.[5]

1. *The capacity to unite love and aggression.* "By uniting our loving emotions with our emotions of anger and hatred, constancy confirms our sense of personal wholeness."

2. *The ability to go on valuing someone even when they no longer provide us with pleasure and satisfaction.* This is the ability to be patient not only with our own bad feelings, but to suffer with others.

3. *The capacity to maintain the wholeness of self and the wholeness of the other.* "Relatedness requires a whole self and a whole other." In this capacity lies the freedom to acknowledge our diversity and differences and even our flaws, rather than splitting from the feared parts of the self.

4. *The capacity to reconcile "our everlasting longings for perfection with our down-to-earth daily existence."* Once we have been accepted as we really are, there is the freedom to set achievable life goals.

Support groups can become a new family working toward this type of wholeness: healthy integration of feelings, commitment to relationships, and acceptance of the self and others. By sharing their struggles honestly, group members can provide human, realistic models for recovery.

Love and Aggression

"I remember that after the first eighteen months of my recovery process, I had a wonderful couple of months." Connie told the group. "I joined the support group for another series and I was still in therapy, but the difference was incredible. Since the whole process started when my old car broke down, it really felt symbolic to me that I had finally saved enough to by a new car! "But as I stood in the shower one morning thinking about a car I had taken for a test drive, I suddenly heard this harsh voice announce, 'You don't deserve a new car!' I freaked out! I thought, 'Oh no! I must be a multiple personality!' I decided to schedule an emergency visit to my therapist and all the way to the office I was imagining myself in the remake of *Sybil!*"

Connie's therapist, however, pointed out that while she had blocked certain memories, she had no history of chronic periods of amnesia or other typical symptoms of a classic case of multiple personality disorder. He explained, however, that in some ways everyone has many "selves" within and he suggested that she was simply becoming aware of another important part of her still fragmented sense of identity.

After working further with her therapist, she recognized the voice she heard in the shower as a parenting, protecting part of her "inner family." "I call this part of me, 'Killer,'" she explained to the group. "Basically this is the part of me that reacted to the incest by saying, 'I am *never* going to let you be abused like that again!'

Killer pulls away from relationships so that I won't get hurt.

"There were a lot of things going on in my life that terrified this part of me. At the time I was planning on buying the new car, I was really enjoying platonic relationships with two men friends. One man was married and the other was dating another woman on a steady basis. Their being unavailable probably gave me confidence to take some risks in getting to know them, but even that much risk drove Killer crazy. He wanted to punish me for breaking the rules—so he told me I didn't 'deserve' a car."

Like most survivors of dysfunctional homes, Connie had a hard time reconciling love and aggression in a healthy way. Either she had no defenses (the "victim" posture) or she had so many that a relationship was impossible. She began to work with her therapist on how to find a middle ground. Predictably, some of these behavior changes caused Killer considerable anxiety.

Wholeness of Self and Others

For Connie, the discovery of her "inner family" of selves grew quickly. In addition to Killer, there was the hurting child of her memories. "The part of me that I recognized when I got into therapy and support group was someone I call 'the Terrified Child.' Sometimes I am overwhelmed with feelings of inferiority, and fear. When I am like this, I just want a tranquilizer and a teddy bear," Connie told the group. "I do not want to talk to anybody or see anybody because if they saw me like this, they would hate me."

Connie's last statement is the central issue: she had

not experienced relationships where others are valued even when they have problems. Like Donna, she had been shamed for her fear and rejected when she reached out. This is what began her inner split with the Terrified Child.

More and more, mental health professionals are coming to the conclusion that "We each consist of a group of 'modular selves,' clusters of related beliefs, feelings and experiences about the world."[6] This means that even for children raised in healthy "good-enough" families, wholeness does not mean having only one inner self, but in accepting *all* inner selves (including negative and unwanted selves) as part of the whole. It is not the inner fragmentation—which is part of being human—but the *denial* of our many inner selves which creates the splitting and loss of wholeness. It is as survivors dare to show the most hated and denied parts of themselves and are met with compassion that recovery takes place and wholeness is achieved.

For Connie, the part of herself she found most difficult to acknowledge was someone she called "Starving Child." "I was doing creative visualization with my therapist, and I kept seeing this scrawny little kid in too big pants that he had to hold up. I felt repelled by him."

She identified the Starving Child with her sexuality. "I have always been terrified of relationships with men," she admits, "and there is a part of me that is starving." Connie found it easy to connect the other parts of herself to the chart in chapter 1. The Terrified Child was isolated by her shaming belief that she was bad and without moral value. Killer was focused on the use of power. Ignoring her inner family members, however, had not saved Connie from their impact. The Terrified

Child had kept her alone and Killer had merely enforced a pattern of self deprivation. Meanwhile, the Starving Child went without nurturance, growing more desperate and more likely to make a disastrous mistake in a sexual relationship.

Moving back to the chart, Connie pointed to the area of connections. "This is the part of me I named 'Crying Child.'" "I can get obsessed with the generations of problems we have in our extended family," she explained, "and become acutely depressed as a result. This really gets in the way of my enjoying life. I don't trust happiness. I wonder, 'How can you be happy when your brother may die of alcoholism?'; or I remember my mother or my sister and their difficulties."

For Connie, the answer lay in making peace with all the parts of herself. "I listen to them all," she said, "but I don't necessarily give them what they want!" she told the group. "You should hear me talk to them! I tell Killer, "Now listen, of course you are upset. After what happened to you, it makes a lot of sense that relationships with men scare you. But it isn't the intimacy that hurts—it's not even the sex that hurts. It is being treated abusively that is scary. We don't have to put up with that any more—but we don't have to live without intimacy either! Both of these men are kind and safe, and I don't have a sexual relationship with them. But Killer, I want you to start letting go and relaxing because one of these days I am going to find the right man. That will be okay because I will be the one making the choice, and I can say 'yes' or 'no.' In the meantime, I am going to practice making choices by choosing to buy a decent car."

"When I feel the Terrified Child taking over, I am just as firm. 'Look honey,' I tell her, 'I can love you even when you feel so scared and unlovable. I believe in the goodness within you. Go ahead and hold the teddy bear and relax. Maybe we should phone Sharon or Kate. They won't be angry at you for being so afraid. On Monday, we have an appointment with the therapist and you can tell him what is making you so scared.'

"When I catch myself holding back on enjoying someone or something, I recognize the Crying Child. She says things like, 'How can you enjoy dessert when a child in the Third World is starving?' Well, I know that it is important to do what I can for starving children and to be sensitive to the Third World. On the other hand, no child will be less hungry if I pass up chocolate cake—and my being a 'martyr' will rob me of a few harmless moments of happiness. In the same way, it does not rob my family when I enjoy my own life—it may even enrich them since it makes me more joyous."

Nourishing the "Starving Child" which Connie identified with her sexuality was the most difficult aspect of her new inner family work. "I have always been so afraid to even look at this part of myself," she explained. I still don't find the Starving Child easy to face. I call him baby names like 'Snook'ums' or 'Lambie Pie'—silly, but it helps somehow.

My therapist also suggested that I give this little guy some help with those falling-down trousers, so I now visualized him wearing a pair of bright red suspenders! I also am doing a few things to be nice to my physical self. I had a massage last week, for example, and I have promised myself that I will take hour-long bubble baths several times a week."

Connie's entrenched patterns of self-hatred and self rejection had continued the abuse far past childhood.

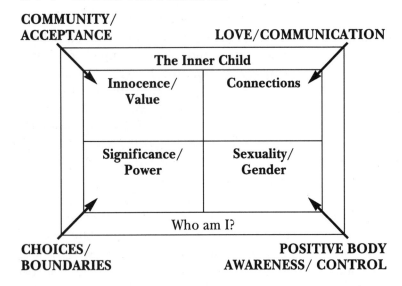

Figure 5. Recovery: The Healing of the Inner Child

Treating herself with kindness—especially the parts of self most often rejected and shamed—is evidence that recovery and wholeness is being achieved. Far from making Connie self-centered, her new understanding gave her new capability to accept others. In fact, others began to seek her out for counsel, instinctively understanding that she would be able to hear the pain they had kept inside.

"For years, I tried so hard to be perfect, to please everyone, to keep my needs from showing, and I felt so fractured," Connie mused. "It's funny that now that I know just how fractured I really am, I feel more at peace than ever before. Not that I feel like I've completely accepted myself or that I don't long for more healing, but I have a new patience with myself and my process. I am beginning to understand that all those parts within have something to teach me."

Wholeness and Our Imperfection

For many readers, it may seem that we have turned the typical understanding of wholeness on its head, and so we have. But this is a kind of wholeness we see reflected in scriptures that reveal the human capacity for pain, evil, and sorrow as well as for great goodness and joy. Indeed, Robert A. Johnson has suggested that looking at the many selves is tolerable only when one presupposes the Nicene Creed, "I believe in One God." He explains, "[The Creed] says that there is only one subject; there is only one Source, one beginning, one unity out of which all the multiplicity of this life flows, and to which it returns. . . . . No matter what tangles and collisions we find within ourselves, they are all branches from one trunk."[9]

While being perfect and nonfragmented is not possible for the individual human soul, we can achieve wholeness in the Eternal Source. "For in Him all things were created, both in the heavens and on earth, visible and invisible . . . and in Him all things hold together" (Col. 1:16–17). This, in the end, is what recovery is all about: the willingness to come to God in our brokenness, trusting in a grace that embraces us as we are and gives meaning to all fragments and wounds and scars.

Acknowledging the depth of our fragmentation and weakness, however, is no simple matter—for survivors of sexual abuse or for anyone else. It is extremely difficult to give up our attempts to be God and to acknowledge our humanity. Accepting that we are not in control of everything usually requires a crisis, a "little death" of self pride. Accepting our limits and our need for God, however, does not leave us in a helpless/hopeless position. On the contrary, people in all types of recovery programs testify that once they have accepted what they cannot control—their past, other people, and so on,—they find a new sense of peace.

"I didn't want to be 'stuck' on sexual abuse my whole life," Donna said. "I wanted to recover. But I found myself constantly obsessing about the past. The sexual abuse happened and I couldn't change that. But I was constantly 'beating up' my Inner Child for talking about it or for making my family unhappy. I was also overwhelmed with guilt that I did not know about Julie's being molested by my ex-husband and worse, that I did not somehow prevent it.

"Then, I went to a conference where the leader brought everyone outside and gave each person a bunch of balloons. She told us to release an unrealistic expectation each time we let go of a balloon and I said, 'I let go of trying to make my memories and gut feelings go away.'

"I waited about three minutes and I released a blue balloon and said, 'I let go of expecting my father to be sorry and apologize.' I released a yellow balloon and said, 'I let go of expecting my mother and sister to understand and support me.'

"I hung on to the rest of the balloons for what felt like forever. Finally, I imagined my daughter standing beside me and I whispered, 'I let go of expecting to be a superhuman mom. I can't always prevent you from being hurt, but I'll always love you, Julie.' Then I let all the rest of the balloons go. I watched them float into the sky and it felt as if an enormous internal weight was gone. I was at peace."

EPILOGUE

As the support group gathered for their last meeting, the atmosphere was easy and talk was punctuated with frequent laughter. The night before, members had held a traditional end-of-group "pajama party." The leaders did not attend; it was a for-members-only function. The only rule, Connie told the group, was *"nobody* talks about incest!" Instead, the party was planned to delight everyone's Inner Child. Plates of brownies, bowls of popcorn, and cans of soda pop decorated the room where the party was held. Stretched out in sleeping bags, the group members told jokes, held long conversations, snapped Polaroid pictures of each other, and watched comedy videos until 2:00 A.M.

"I spent all of my childhood wishing I would be invited to parties like this!" Alice told the group that night. "Now that I know how much fun they are, I may just spend my retirement in my pajamas!" At the meeting the next day, Donna presented her with a pair of flannel "retirement pajamas," complete with sewn-in feet and a back flap. The group exploded in laughter and applause while Alice held the outfit against her and took a bow.

After three months, the communication between the seven women had become natural, almost intuitive.

"I've never had a group of friends I knew this well," Kate said. "I've spent my whole life trying to fake friendship, trying to keep people from knowing me. I can't tell you what this has meant." As each person shared how the group had helped her, the feelings were unanimous. "I needed to know I wasn't alone," Ruth said simply.

Not all groups are as successful at bonding as this one. But most give members at least a taste of the "holding environment" so necessary to enable young children to develop trust. Of course, the lack of a nurturing family in childhood is not something that can be made up for in ten-week sessions. Such a support group is only one step on the road to recovery, but it can be a step of enormous importance.

As group members talked during the last session, it was clear that even at this stage of recovery many of them were trying out new patterns of behavior drawn from the group experience. Several were trying mourning prayers and/or grieving journals on their own. All were working hard in therapy and Ruth had added special joint therapy sessions with her daughter. All seven of the group members reported that they were handling relationships in new ways.

Even if they were unclear about the why of their suffering, they believed that they had learned a tremendous amount about themselves and others by walking through the pain together. The reframing of recovery was happening on an almost daily basis. "Still," Kate said, "I sometimes feel like I am back at square one. A dream or a memory can send me on a tailspin emotionally. Will I ever be normal?" Kate is still in the beginning stages of recovery, and to some degree her sensitivity to this pain will lessen (particularly as she shares it), but it is unlikely that it will ever be completely gone.

The healing process itself is a series of recovery stages. It is not unusual for incest survivors to need intense assistance for about two years, ideally through the three avenues outlined in chapter 9 (therapy; support group; inner work). At the end of the first three-month term, five of the women in the group—Kate, Donna, Alice, Sharon, and Ruth—planned to join a support group for a second term. Connie, who had been attending support groups for several terms, accepted a position as a group coleader. Gerri, however, decided on at least a temporary break from support group. She had been briefly readmitted to the hospital the week before when additional difficult memories had surfaced. The severity of her reaction convinced her to join a daily outpatient program based at the hospital. This included more ongoing individual and group work than a support group and weekly therapy could provide. "The support group was helpful," Gerri explained, "but I think I'll benefit from it more in a few months, after I've had more professional help."

It is especially difficult for survivors to cope with the phenomenon that Kate described and Gerri experienced—the sense of being "back at square one." At discouraging moments like this, it makes a tremendous difference to put those feelings in perspective. Three tools are especially useful:

1. A file of inner work (prayers, journal notes, and so on) can remind the survivor of insights gained and small victories won. "One night I was back in full-fledged denial," Donna told the group. "I was

convinced that I had imagined everything. I pulled out my journals, looked at my drawings and at the notes I had made after I talked to my aunt and the other two girls at the school where my dad worked. The adult part of me sat and read through all of this and realized that the evidence was all there."

2. The group's ability to mirror or reflect back to the survivor just how far she really has come can be critical in helping to overcome her feelings of discouragement. A therapist can also function as a reality check when the survivor loses sight of the real progress that she made.

3. The example of someone further along in the process can be very encouraging. "I still have moments of deep depression and anger," Connie told the group, "but the intensity is far less than what I felt the first eighteen or twenty months after my memories surfaced. Also, I know what to do when the feelings come up. The distress may not have gone away completely—maybe it never will on some levels—but I don't feel as lost."

As Connie explained, sexual abuse leaves emotional and spiritual marks even after the trauma has been reframed. Healing is possible; becoming as if it had never happened may not be. Instead, recovery can come through accepting—even embracing—those scars, becoming what Henri Nouwen termed a "wounded healer."

Jesus was just such a healer. He carried the scars of his wounds even after the Resurrection. He had recovered from death itself, yet his shameful execution was advertised in the unsightly marks on his body. In fact, he used them to establish his identity: "Reach here your finger and see my hands; and reach here your hand, and put it into my side; and be not unbelieving, but believing" (John 20:27). The meaning of those scars had changed. He was no longer the victim of evil. He was the triumphant Christ.

The scars of sexual betrayal can also change their meaning when they are openly shared with a community of faith. Eventually, those scars become the most powerful evidence of what has been survived, an enduring testimony to hope.

Appendix 1

SUGGESTIONS FOR SURVIVORS
OF SEXUAL ABUSE

Listening to survivors of child sexual abuse actively choose the path to recovery never failed to inspire us as authors. We applaud the courage of every survivor who stands poised on the brink of that decision. The following suggestions for pursuing recovery are drawn from the experience of listening to and working with the many women who are part of the VIRTUES network.

1. Find a qualified therapist with experience in child sexual abuse treatment. It is not essential that your therapist share your particular theological perspective, although you may find that helpful. It is critical, however, that you feel safe in that therapeutic relationship. Don't be afraid to change therapists or to interview several until you find one who can help you on your journey to recovery. For further suggestions see "Shopping for Help" at the end of this section.

2. Find a support group that can walk with you through your recovery process. If you are just beginning your own recovery, it is *not* advisable for you to begin or lead a new support group. It is easy for a survivor to get caught up in organizing a group and helping others at

the very moment that the primary focus should remain on her own wholeness.

Instead, check community resources for an already existing group. Almost all do not charge fees for membership. Groups like VIRTUES cover both the emotional and spiritual issues of incest survival. A secular survivors' group can also give you the vital support you need for recovery. VOICES has chapters throughout the United States. Parents United, an international organization, also sponsors Adults Molested as Children support groups. See the section entitled "Self-Help and Support Group Resources" at the end of this book for information on how to contact these groups.

If your community does not have a support group for the survivors of child sexual abuse, you should seriously consider attending the meetings of one of the twelve-step groups for codependents. SA-Anon, for example focuses on codependent responses to sexually addictive and abusive behaviors. Even if your family's particular issue was not alcohol or food addiction, you will find that Al-Anon; Adult Children of Alcoholics; Overeaters Anonymous, and other programs will give you helpful insights into your family dynamic. Most twelve-step groups share an emphasis on support and recovery is very helpful.

If you have an active addiction to alcohol, drugs, and/or sexually abusive behavior, we encourage you to wait until you have been in an addiction recovery program for at least one year before joining a survivor support group. Instead, consider an appropriate twelve-step program: Alcoholics Anonymous; Overcomers Outreach; Cocaine Anonymous; Sexual Addicts Anonymous, etc. These groups are also listed under "Self-Help and Support Group Resources" at the end of this book.

3. Once you have a support network in place, begin your inner work in discovering the child within. Writing exercises (journaling, recording dreams, dialoguing with the Inner Child), artistic expression (painting, working with clay), active imagery, and prayer all have a place in this process. Remember, however, that inner work can turn up powerful material, and make sure that there are people you can contact (including your therapist and support group members) if you need support.

"Shopping for Help:"
How to Find a Competent Counselor or
Therapist*
By Bethyl Joy Shepperson, Psy.D.

1. What is important to you?

   Professional Skills—Speciality area, education, licensing and credentials, training and experience in child sexual abuse treatment
   Personal Skills—Someone who can:
       hear you
       respect you
       tune into your strengths as well as liabilities,
   and
       —Someone who has:
       the ability to support
       the ability to confront

   Preferences—Do you have any preferences about age, gender, and other related issues?

   Openness—If the therapist is not experienced with the issues important to you then she or he should be open to learning from you and other professionals about these issues.

   Other Things to Consider—Cost and the availability of third-party payments (insurance), how far you want to travel, appointment scheduling.

2. Ask for referrals from respected friends and/or

---

*Adapted from and reproduced with permission

those who were in therapy and were satisfied with their experience.

3. Ask for referrals from your minister, doctor, school psychologist, teachers, or other professionals.

4. Look in the phone book under counseling, marriage counseling, psychologists. Call around.

5. If you can't afford the standard fee for therapy, consider:
   a. Colleges with master's degree programs in counseling often have graduate students who do counseling under supervision of licensed therapist.
   b. Some clinics offer internships to graduate students who work at a lower fee and under the supervision of a licensed practitioner.
   c. State and county mental health associations offer low cost therapy.

6. Once you find some qualified counselors/therapists, find out if they fit your needs.
   a. Review the points important to you.
   b. Can this therapist be supportive and respectful of a person with strong religious beliefs? Is it important to you that your therapist be a Christian? Do you expect the counselor to provide both emotional and spiritual support?

SUGGESTIONS FOR
CHURCH LEADERS

Churches are in an ideal position to provide the community support needed by the survivors of child sexual abuse. Most seminaries and Christian education programs, however, do not provide training on dealing with incestous families or information on the recovery of adults molested as children. This ministry requires individual commitment and preparation on the part of pastors, priests, pastoral counselors and lay leaders.

The following suggestions provide some helpful ideas on how church leaders can actively support recovery from the emotional and spiritual traumas of child sexual abuse.

1. Become educated about child sexual abuse; take advantage of seminars, videotapes, and other resources that are specifically aimed at the clergy. Make sure the church staff is up to date on the mandatory reporting of child sexual abuse in your state. Recent legal decisions indicate that church leaders may be included in laws requiring that professionals report sexual abuse disclosures to the civil authorities.

2. Create links with the professional mental health community and find contacts for referrals of church

members. If your church is interested in beginning a support group ministry for survivors, find a qualified professional—perhaps a member of your own church— who could supervise and advise support group leaders.

3. Survivors of child sexual abuse often face serious depression that needs professional attention. A recovery model that combines individual therapy and inner work with a support group offers tremendous advantages. Support group membership alone should not be expected to provide all of the help most survivors need. The most effective way to set up a support group ministry, in our opinion, is to require that each group member also receive individual therapy. The church may want to set up a special scholarship program to assist survivors in paying for professional help and a referral list of qualified therapists.

This model, in addition to effectively promoting recovery for survivors, also provides tremendous advantages to the church leadership team. First of all, they do not have the whole burden of facilitating recovery; they have a professional partner working individually with the survivor. Knowing the survivor's therapist can be notified if there is a suicide threat or other indication of serious problems gives a volunteer ministry professional backup as well as providing a legal safeguard for the church. The organizing leadership team needs to set up a church-based program that is clearly a support ministry and not a mental health treatment program; otherwise there is an increased risk of burnout, misunderstanding, and/or legal suits.

4. Establish and respect anonymity and confidentiality. While a long-range goal is for survivors to feel

comfortable attending their own church's group, many will prefer—at least at first—to attend a group at another church. In any case, it should always be up to the individual survivor to identify herself or himself as a group member. If records are kept, they should only be used by the group's leader and not filed with general church records.

5. Be cautious about using Scripture as a "band-aid" response to the deep-seated problems caused by child sexual abuse. Insensitive but well-meaning church leaders have caused survivors much emotional turmoil by suggesting the abuse be forgotten or insisting that forgiveness be instant.

THE VIRTUES PROGRAM

Statement of Purpose:

VIRTUES is a program of recovery based on the acronym: *Victims of Incest Recover through Understanding, Education and Support.* It is designed to help adult survivors come to a deeper understanding of their unique value as human beings and of their worth before God. VIRTUES was developed in 1987 by a group of Christian women who, by walking together through their own pain, created a healing community. Support groups grew out of their loving concern for others ensnared in the vicious cycle of guilt and shame which separated them from healthy relationships with God and others. VIRTUES attempts to restore dignity to individuals who have experienced the excruciating humiliation of incest and assist them in their struggle for identity and healthy self-esteem. VIRTUES groups meet for three ten-week sessions a year. Professionally supervised counselors and survivors guide the small support groups to create an atmosphere of confidentiality and safety where childhood feelings and experiences can be identified and validated between group members.

Recommended Recovery Model

We strongly recommend that survivors of child sexual abuse pursue all three of the following avenues to healing, particularly during the first twelve to twenty-four months of recovery: (1) therapy with a qualified professional who has experience in child sexual abuse treatment; (2) membership in VIRTUES or a similar support or self-help group; and (3) inner work (journaling, prayer, meditation, painting, and so forth) that facilitates self expression and growth.

The Role of the VIRTUES Support Group in Recovery

Support Versus Therapy

The VIRTUES system is organized to provide support rather than therapy. Support groups and therapy groups overlap in many areas. Both emphasize the freedom to express all feelings, experiences, and beliefs in an accepting atmosphere. However, some significant differences in the focus and goals of support groups make them distinct from group therapy.

The support group's main function is to create a nurturing family atmosphere where healthy connections and communication can take place. The emphasis is bonding and socialization rather than confrontive therapeutic intervention. The probing and pushing that is appropriate within a therapy group contrasts with the more gentle and supportive role of a VIRTUES group.

The major healing power of these groups lies in the emphasis upon acceptance, love, and honesty. Despite the low-key nature of support groups, the intensity of dealing with memories of child sexual abuse is potent. Inevitably, group members discover that they are reacting to others as if they were their parents or siblings, projecting their old attachments and conflicts into this new group. Within the support group, however, the issues can be addressed and resolved—something that may not have been possible in their dysfunctional home. In this way, the support group provides a *safe place* for group members to try out new and healthy behaviors and to show parts of themselves they have discovered in therapy or in their own inner journey. It is this healthy, loving bond with others that is the core of support.

Safe Places/Safe People

Meeting in a church will not insure that the support group is a safe place. Safe places require safe people who can create a healthy atmosphere of acceptance. While the emphasis should be upon freedom of expression, safety also requires defined limits and boundaries.

"In the nurturing family," Virginia Satir has written, "it is easy to pick up the message that human life and human feelings are more important than anything else."[1] It is this message that makes an environment safe. The following guidelines for support group rules are adapted from Satir's ingredients for nurturing families:

Safe Place Rules for VIRTUES Groups

1. Members are free to tell each other how they feel.

2. Each person knows she will have a chance to be heard.

3. Members are comfortable touching one another

appropriately (hugs, squeezing a hand, and the like) but it is always okay to ask *not* to be touched.

4. The emphasis is upon being direct and real with one another.

5. Conflicts are resolved, not avoided.

6. There is a consistent focus on valuing one another and respecting each other's feelings.

Goals for VIRTUES Support Groups

1. *Love.* The loving acceptance of each group member is unconditional.

2. *Sharing.* Telling and retelling the story, expressing feelings about past and present experiences and overcoming denial are primary tasks for the support group meetings.

3. *Mastery.* Each member is in charge of when and if she will share her feelings and/or story. Making choices is a learned skill and it is critical that the survivor have a sense of power or mastery in her own recovery. Each member is accepted wherever she is in the recovery process; there is no push to "hurry up and get in touch with all of your memories."

4. *Boundaries.* Survivors are encouraged to stop blaming themselves for their victimization as children. Instead, there is encouragement to take responsibility for their own recovery as adults. Learning what appropriate boundaries are can be

facilitated by leaders who offer support without taking inappropriate responsibility for others.

5. *Trust.* Appropriate trust for others and God is encouraged through modeling a trustworthy, nurturing "family" atmosphere.

The Leadership Team

Attitude

Choosing the right leadership team for a support group is critical to its success. It is essential to choose people who have worked through their own grieving process (whether their pain involved child sexual abuse or some other loss). These "wounded healers" need to be farther along in their recovery process than the group members, since they serve as role models and surrogate parents. Effective leaders do not, however, see themselves as the "healthy" ones in contrast to the "sick" group members. These leaders' have an awareness of their own scars and the ongoing nature of their own recovery.

Abilities

1. The ability to appreciate differences,

2. The ability to tolerate and resolve conflicts,

3. The ability to value others—leaders and group members,

4. The ability to show compassion,

5. The ability to be expressive in an open, direct, and respectful manner,

6. The ability to display empathy rather than sympathy,

7. The ability to see through "soft eyes," reflecting respect and nurturing acceptance rather than criticism and judgment,

8. The ability to show brokenness, admitting failures, fears, and weakness,

9. The ability to laugh at oneself,

10. The ability to communicate to others (through attitude, action, and words) a healthy concept of God.

Integrating Professionals and Recovering Survivors in Ministry

The VIRTUES leadership team includes mental health professionals and recovering survivors committed to using their spiritual gifts in a church setting. Both groups contribute greatly to the program's success:

Leading or supervising a VIRTUES support group allows mental health professional to donate their time to an important effort which integrates their skills and professional training. For some counselors, this ministry can provide an important connection between their Christian service and their professional career.

Support group leadership also can provide a deeply fulfilling experience for recovering survivors. Many graduates of the VIRTUES support system have become successful group leaders. Their presence and continued healing provides a much needed testimony that recovery can and does occur even in people terribly wounded in childhood. It is interesting that several of these gifted lay leaders have decided to expand their ministry by becoming professionals and are now pursuing degrees in some area of mental health.

Boundaries

Whether professional or nonprofessional, support group leaders must model in their own lives—and in group—appropriate boundaries. Taking care of oneself, caring for others without taking responsibility for them, maintaining one's own spiritual growth, and communicating directly are all skills that require the continuing attention of every leader. Codependent helpers, in the end, can damage the recovery process. An important safeguard against becoming overly responsible for others is to find places where one is encouraged to share one's particular fears and concerns and shed the role of leader.

For this reason, VIRTUES leaders meet together once a month for their own support group and for clinical supervision. Leaders also take the time annually to go on a retreat together.

Suggested Format for Support Group Meetings

First Meeting: Basic Format

1. Welcome to the group.

2. Explain the dynamics of the group:
   a. Explain *support vs. therapy* and the creation of a healthy family model. Note the requirement that members be in therapy while participating in support group.

b. Group rules:
   1. Purpose: To talk about ourselves and to explore our feelings.
   2. Boundaries: No taking responsibility for others or advice giving; the focus remains on one's own recovery process.

3. Explain the *safe places model and safe people characteristics* (see "Safe Places/Safe People" earlier in this appendix).

4. Create a *group covenant* (see "The Support Group Covenant" later in this appendix).

5. *Confidentiality:* Stress that what is said in the group remains in group, and that group membership is anonymous. This is a principle that group leaders and group members alike should affirm.

6. *Limits of confidentiality:* Distribute and explain the Limits of Confidentiality and Authorization of Disclosure contracts, included later in this appendix.

7. *Attendance:* Explain that group members should attend all ten sessions. A member should notify the group leader if she cannot attend a session, but such absence should be avoided. Attendance is a critical part of the group recovery process and of building bonding and trust within the support group. A member who does not take this commitment seriously will trigger the group's feelings of betrayal and abandonment.

8. *Sharing:*
   a. Each coleader tells the group about her own journey (this provides an opportunity to model the openness and honesty allowed in the group).
   b. Group members introduce themselves.

    c. Coleaders ask for any questions about the group program.

9. *Closing:* It is important that meetings begin and end on time. A suggested meeting length is one and a half hours. This is an important boundary issue. This schedule allows the coleaders and group members to put a reasonable limit on their commitment and mutual responsibility. Groups that consistently violate such time limits to be helpful to those who still have issues to discuss may simply reinforce codependency.

Some groups may wish to end with a moment of silent meditation, or a leader may read a brief poem, essay, scripture, or prayer. Some groups ask volunteers from the group to say sentence prayers as a closing; be careful, however, that this does not become an awkward, forced exercise where members feel compelled to perform. One variation would be to lead the group in a relaxation exercise and have the coleaders close with a brief prayer. The focus is on inner quiet and letting go of the pain expressed in the group.

Next Nine Meetings

Different leaders and groups create their own style and formats, particularly as the weeks go on. Most groups spend at least a couple of sessions on having members tell the story of their abuse within this supportive community. A good basic structure for the additional sessions includes the following elements:

1. *Check-in time* (approximately five minutes per group member): Where are you today in terms of your feelings, your issues, your memories? What do you need from the group today?

2. *Personal Sharing:* A group leader may ask, "Who would like to share first today?" A group member may volunteer her story or unfinished business from last week's group meeting.

3. *Response:* The group responds to each member's expressed need and/or story.

4. *Closing:* See suggestions on closing of first meeting.

The Support Group Covenant

Support groups must be safe places to be effective in helping the survivors of child sexual abuse move toward recovery. People who have been raised in abusive families, however, find it especially difficult to feel safe and it is important to respect and respond to those concerns.

One excellent method for establishing the right environment for trust is the creation of a covenant among the members of the support group. This concept was introduced by Dr. Beth Shepperson, the clinical supervisor for VIRTUES.

The covenant is begun by having the support group leader ask the group, "What do you need from the group to make this a safe place?" The group's answers are written on a large poster. Answers that have been given in the past have included:

"It has to be okay to cry—let's keep a good supply of Kleenex!"

"No censorship—I have got to say what I really feel."

"No shame and no judgment—I want people to look at me with 'soft eyes'!"

"I need some hugs."

"I want the freedom to let my Inner Child show."

"I want to know that you can be trusted—that you won't talk to others about what I say in group."

"I want respect."

Once the responses have been written on the poster, it can be passed around for everyone's signature (use first names only, or initials or even pseudonyms). This covenant seals the group's commitment to keeping the support group safe for every member.

Limits of Confidentiality

The Limits of Confidentiality form is distributed, filled out and returned during the first support group meeting. The VIRTUES group leader keeps these forms on file. To protect the privacy of group members, the Limits of Confidentiality forms and the Authorization of Disclosure forms are not filed with general church office files.

The VIRTUES Support Group of _____
Church is a group established to help facilitate the healing process of your own personal therapy through the love, support, and encouragement of women who share an experience similar to your own. We are a support group and not a therapy group. Your primary healing will take place through the work you are doing with your therapist. The VIRTUES Support Group will enhance the healing process by providing you a safe and supportive environment in which to share. Sharing in this group will remain confidential. However, there are certain limits to confidentiality within this group:

1. Confidentiality must be set aside if your facilitator has reasonable cause to believe that a group member is a danger to herself or others.

2. If your facilitator is a mandated reporter, by law, she must report cases of sexual, physical, or emotional child abuse or neglect.

3. Confidentiality is based on cooperation of all group members to maintain it. However, the facilitators have no power to enforce what a group member chooses to

(continued)

do outside of the group. If a member chooses to break the confidence of any member sharing in the group, she may jeopardize her membership in the group, because the ability to keep a confidence is one of the requirements for group membership.

4. During group supervision, your facilitators may share some of the group processes with their supervisor in order to receive instruction, guidance, and direction for your benefit and that of the group.

I have read and understand the limits of confidentiality for the VIRTUES Support Group of _____ Church. I will respect and keep the confidences of the group members as shared with me inside the group.

Signed _____

Date _____

Authorization of Disclosure

Two copies of the Authorization of Disclosure form should be given to each group member during the first session. After completing the forms, each group member should ask her therapist to sign both copies. The therapist may keep one copy of the form. The group member should return the second signed copy to the group leader at the next group meeting.

I, _____ , hereby authorize the mutual exchange of information pertaining to myself and my participation in the VIRTUES (Victims of Incest Recover Through Understanding, Education, and Support) Support Group of _____ Church between the following persons/agencies:

VIRTUES Support Group _____Church

Therapist Name: _____
Address: _____
City: _____
Phone Number: _____

Cofacilitators: _____
_____
Address: _____
Phone Number: _____
_____

I understand that this information will pertain to any behavioral changes observed by the cofacilitators and/or

(continued)

therapist that are of concern to them, or to discussion of whether or not my participation in the group at this time will be beneficial to my healing process.

I am currently the client of the above psychotherapist and will be attending therapy sessions on a regular basis during the period of _____ through _____.

Date: _____

_____
(Signature of client)

Exp. Date of Release: _____

_____
(Signature of witness)

_____
(Signature of therapist, including license number)

Photocopies of this form are acceptable.

NOTES

Prologue

1. Renita J. Weems sermon, "Cry, Baby Cry: The Weeping Women of Jeremiah" was our first introduction to this powerful example of women's ministry in scripture. The sermon was presented by Dr. Weems as part of The Women's Lectureship at Fuller Seminary, April 22, 1987.

Chapter 1: Discovery of the Lost Child

1. Alice Miller, *The Drama of the Gifted Child* (New York: Basic Books, 1981).
2. Several researchers have noted the connection between incest and a negative self-image. See S. M. Sgroi, "A Conceptual Framework for Child Sexual Abuse," *Handbook of Clinical Intervention in Child Sexual Abuse* (Lexington, MA: Lexington Books, 1982), and M. Tsai and N. N. Wagner, "Therapy Groups for Women Molested as Children, *Archives of Sexual Behavior* 7 (1978): 417–427. A comprehensive look at the long-term impact of child sexual abuse is found in Diana E. H. Russell's *The Secret Trauma: Incest in the Lives of Girls and Women* (New York: Basic Books, 1986).
3. Two very useful models for understanding the development of self-esteem include those used in Stanley Coopersmith's *The Antecedents of Self-Esteem* (San Francisco: W. H. Freeman, 1967) and Linda Sanford and Mary Ellen Donovan's *Women and Self-Esteem* (New York: Penguin Books, 1984). Coopersmith names four components of success in establishing a sense of self (p. 38): power, virtue, significance, and competence. Sanford and Donovan suggest five elements (p. 38): a sense of significance, a sense of competence, a sense of connectedness to others balanced by a sense of separateness from them, a sense of

realism about ourselves and the world, and a coherent set of ethics and values.

4. David Finkelhor and Anela Browne, "The Traumatic Impact of Child Sexual Abuse: A Conceptualization," *American Journal of Orthopsychiatry* 55 (1984): 530–541.

5. Claudia Black, *It Will Never Happen to Me* (Denver: M.A.C. Printing and Publications Division, 1981).

6. Miller, *Gifted Child*, p. 67.

7. Arthur Miller, *After the Fall* (New York: Viking Press, 1964), p. 21.

8. "True mourning ends with what is called internalization, a 'taking in' of the person who was lost to us." Maggie Scarf applies this description of the mourning process both to the psychological separation from and "loss" of parents and to the loss of the child self in adolescence, in her book *Unfinished Business* (New York: Ballantine Books, 1980), pp. 31–32.

9. Louise J. Kaplan, *Oneness and Separateness: From Infant to Individual* (New York: Simon & Schuster, 1978), p. 45.

Chapter 2: The Survivor and Shame

1. Using hypnosis to retrieve buried memories is an area of concern and controversy. Some therapists believe that hypnosis can prematurely release memories which need to stay repressed until the client has built enough ego strength to cope with a traumatic event. Many clinicians stressed to us that survivors do not have to have detailed recall of abusive incidents in order to recover.

   Survivors should not even consider hypnosis unless their therapist is fully qualified in this area. The therapist should be able to show evidence of successful completion of accredited course work in hypnosis and supervised experience in a clinical setting. Connie's therapist was a licensed counselor who met these criteria.

2. Bernie Siegel, *Peace, Love, and Healing* (New York: Harper & Row, 1989), p. 115.

3. "In a sense, the child kills his or her own feelings, wishes, and demands in order to preserve the bond with the narcissistic parent. This leads to a sense of 'false self' with the 'true self' being 'in a state of noncommunication' because it has to be protected," writes the Reverend Susan Konkel, M.A., M. Div., in her unpublished paper, "Shame Faced," submitted to the faculty of the California Family Study Center, October 22, 1988. We are especially grateful to Sue for her insights and encouragement as we developed this theme in our chapter.

Healing the Shame That Binds You by John Bradshaw (Deerfield Beach, FL: Health Communications, 1988), *Facing Shame: Families in Recovery* by M. A. Fossum and M. J. Mason (New York: W. W. Norton, 1986), and *Shame: The Power of Caring* by G. Kaufman (Cambridge, MA: Schenkman, 1985) are recommended to readers interested in further information on the concept of shame.

4. Abraham Maslow, *Toward a Psychology of Being*, 2nd ed. (Princeton: Van Nostrand, 1968), p. 8.

5. This incident is often confused with a similar passage in which a prostitute weeps for her sins at Jesus' feet, wipes the tears away with her hair, and anoints his feet with perfume. Jesus responds to this woman by forgiving her sins (this story is recorded in Luke 7:36–50). In fact, however, this is a very different stituation. Mary was a well-known disciple from a prominent family and not a prostitute. Moreover, there is no mention of sins or forgiveness in the Bethany stories and no mention of death or burial in the prostitute's story.

Chapter 3: The Survivor and Family

1. Roland Summit, M.D., "Too Terrible to Hear," Testimony before the Attorney General's Commission on Pornography, Miami, FL. November 20, 1985, pp. 2–3.

2. "The more distant the relationship, the more supportive the reaction (significant at >0.01 level)." Russell, *Secret Trauma*, p. 358.

3. Many survivors have told us that the insights in Lewis Smedes, *Forgive and Forget* (San Francisco: Harper & Row, 1984) were extremely helpful in understanding the difference between forgiveness and mere forgetfulness.

4. Nicholas Groth and Ann Burgess, "Sexual Trauma in the Life History of Rapists and Child Molesters," *Victimology* 4 (1979) pp. 10–16.

5. Toni Cavanagh Johnson, "Female Child Perpetrators: Children Who Molest Other Children," *Child Abuse and Neglect* 13 (1989) pp. 571–585.

6. Toni Cavanagh Johnson, "Child Perpetrators—Children Who Molest Other Children: Preliminary Findings," *Child Abuse and Neglect* 12 (1988). pp. 219–229.

Chapter 4: The Survivor and Sexuality

1. American Psychiatric Association, *Diagnostic and Statistical Manual of Mental Disorders* (Washington, D.C., APA, 1980) p. 236.

2. Sanford and Donovan, *Women and Self-Esteem*, p. 13.
3. Researcher David Finkelhor found no connection between childhood victimization and adult homosexual activity for girls, although "boys victimized by older men were over *four times* more likely to be currently engaged in homosexual activities than were nonvictims. Close to half the male respondents who had had a childhood sexual experience with an older man were currently involved in homosexual activity." *Child Sexual Abuse: New Theory and Research* (New York: Macmillan, 1984), p. 195.

   Diana Russell did not ask respondents in her study for sexual preference but noted, "Some data outside of our survey, as well as clinical evidence, suggest that one response to the trauma of incest is to turn away from heterosexuality and to embrace a lesbian orientation and life style. If such a relationship between incest and lesbianism exists, given the prevalence of homophobia in this society, this would indeed be evidence of the trauma of incest. Whether or not this outcome is viewed positively or negatively, however, is entirely a matter of opinion" (*Secret Trauma*, pp. 199–200).

   Additional information on sexual orientation and its connection to sexual abuse is included in *Incest and Sexuality, A Guide to Understanding and Healing* by Wendy Maltz and Beverly Holman (Lexington, MA: 1987) pp. 72–74.
4. Johnson, "Female Child Perpetrators."
5. Groth and Burgess, *Sexual Trauma*.
6. Interview (June 1987) with Dr. Karin Meiselman, author of *Incest: A Psychological Study of Causes and Effects with Treatment Recommendations* (San Francisco: Jossey-Bass, 1978).
7. Ibid.
8. Ibid.

Chapter 5: The Survivor and Power

1. It may be difficult for some readers to believe that an 11-year-old boy would be capable of rape, but research is beginning to emerge on incidents like the one Alice reported. The studies by Toni Cavanagh Johnson (cited earlier) are the first reports published on children who molest younger children. These boys and girls (aged 4–13 years) had forced sexual behaviors that sometimes included intercourse, sodomy, oral sex, or penetration with a foreign object. In almost half of the cases, their victims were younger members of the immediate family.

2. John Bradshaw, *Bradshaw on the Family: A Revolutionary Way of Self-Discovery* (Deerfield Beach, FL: Health Communications, 1988), pp 131–132.
3. Morton Kelsey, *Caring: How Can We Love One Another?* (New York: Paulist Press, 1981), p. 18.

Chapter 6: The Survivor and Prayer

1. Carl Jung, *Modern Man in Search of a Soul* (New York: Harcourt Brace Jovanovich, 1933), p. 229.
2. Pierre Wolff, *May I Hate God?* (New York: Paulist Press, 1979), p. 32.
3. "Many, if not most, victims are sexually abused in ways that leave no lasting physical indicators." MacFarlane and Feldmeth, *Response*, p. 3.
4. Dietrich Bonhoeffer, *Letters and Papers from Prison* (New York: Macmillan, 1953, 1967, 1971), p. 348.

Chapter 7: The Survivor and God

1. Roberta Nobleman, "Call It Not Love," *The Witness Magazine*, April 1988 (Ambler, PA: Episcopal Church Publishing Co.), p. 21.
2. Kari Torjesen Malcolm introduced us to the concept that ignoring the multiple biblical images of God in favor of only the "Father" picture is a form of idolatry as well as sexism. She developed this theme in "Christian Women at the Crossroads," presented at the First Presbyterian church, Sherman Oaks, California, March 8, 1986.
3. An excellent resource for these images is *The Divine Feminine: The Biblical Imagery of God as Female* by Virginia Ramey Mollenkott (New York: Crossroad, 1984).
4. A caution should be added, however, that even therapeutic and pastoral relationships are not automatically 'safe' and survivors may be especially vulnerable to sexual victimization by authority figures. Two helpful resources in establishing guidelines are *Professional Therapy Never Includes Sex* by Valerie Quinn (Sacramento: Board of Behavioral Science Examiners, California Department of Consumer Affairs, 1990) and *Is Nothing Sacred? The Betrayal of a Pastoral Relationship* by Marie Fortune (San Francisco: Harper & Row, 1989).
5. Cedric Johnson, *Religion That Hurts Too Much* (unpublished manuscript, 1988).

6. C. S. Lewis, *A Grief Observed* (London: Faber & Faber, 1961), p. 26.
7. Ibid, pp. 27–28.

Chapter 8: The Survivor and Evil

1. David Finkelhor, Linda Meyer Williams with Nanci Burns, *Nursery Crimes: Sexual Abuse in Day Care* (Newbury Park, CA: Sage Publications, 1988), pp. 59–60.
2. Laura Kagy, "Ritualized Abuse of Children," *Recap* (Columbus, OH: National Child Assault Prevention Project, Winter 1985), p. 1
3. Finkelhor, *Nursery Crimes*, pp. 62–63.
4. Kagy, "Ritualized Abuse of Children," p. 1.
5. Dee Brown, "The Nature of the Assault," *Ritual Abuse: General Information* (Los Angeles: Children's Institute International, 1988), p. 31.
6. Finkelhor, *Nursery Crimes*, p. 61.
7. Brown, "The Nature of the Assault," p. 31.
8. Finkelhor, *Nursery Crimes*, p. 64.
9. Scott Peck, in *People of the Lie* (New York: Simon & Schuster, 1983), has stressed that even people who have had deliverances perceived as successful require intensive follow-up care and ongoing therapy.
10. We are indebted to our friend and colleague, Earl Henslin, Psy. D., for this insight, which explains the sense of spiritual invasion by evil experiences by survivors who were repeatedly—but not ritually—abused.
11. Frederick Buechner, "Wishful Thinking," *A Theological ABC* (New York: Harper & Row, Publishers 1973) p.47.
12. Scott Peck, *People of the Lie*, p. 129.
13. Ibid. p. 130.
14. Marie Fortune, "Forgiveness: The Last Step," *Abuse and Religion: When Praying Isn't Enough* (Lexington, MA: Lexington Books, 1988) p. 218–19.

Chapter 9: The Survivor and Forgiveness

1. David Augsburger, *Caring Enough to Forgive/Caring Enough Not to Forgive* (Ventura, CA: Regal Books, 1981), Part 2, p. 52.
2. Dr. Ken Magid and Carole A. McKelvey, *High Risk: Children Without a Conscience* (New York: Bantam Books, 1987), p. 74.

3. The concept of the "good enough" mother was developed by D. W. Winnicott. "The Theory of the Parent-Infant Relationship," in *The Maturational Process and the Facilitating Environment* (New York: I.U.P., 1960).
4. An excellent and understandable introduction to genograms is Emily Martin's *Genograms: The New Tool for Exploring the Personality, Career and Love Patterns You Create* (Chicago: Contemporary Books, 1989).

Chapter 10: The Survivor and Wholeness

1. Irving Yalom, *Love's Executioner* (New York: Harper & Row, 1989), p. 12.
2. Louise J. Kaplan, Ph.D., *Oneness and Separateness* (New York: Simon & Schuster, 1978). We are grateful to clinical psychologist Joyce Hulgus for introducing us to the writings of Kaplan, and for encouraging us to integrate developmental needs with the recovery process in our writing.
3. Renita J. Weems, *Just A Sister Away: A Womanist Vision of Women's Relationships in the Bible* (San Diego: LuraMedia, 1988), p. 60.
4. Scott Peck's *The Different Drum: Community Making and Peace* (New York: Simon & Schuster, 1987) is an excellent resource on creating communities and dealing with group resistance to process.
5. Kaplan, *Oneness and Separateness*, p. 46.
6. Richard Schwartz, Ph.D., "Our Multiple Selves," *Family Therapy Networker* magazine, March/April 1987, p. 26.
7. Robert A. Johnson, *Inner Work* (San Francisco: Harper & Row, 1986), p. 37.

Appendix 3

1. Virginia Satir, *Peoplemaking* (Palo Alto, CA: Science and Behavior Books, 1972).

RECOMMENDED READING
AND RESOURCES

Recommended Reading

Child Sexual Abuse

Bass, Ellen, and Davis, Laura. *The Courage to Heal: A Guide for Women Survivors of Child Sexual Abuse.* New York: Harper & Row, 1988.

Crewdson, John. *By Silence Betrayed: Sexual Abuse of Children in America.* Boston: Little, Brown, 1988.

Forward, Susan, and Buck, Craig. *Betrayal of Innocence.* Los Angeles: J. P. Tarcher, 1978.

Frank, Jan. *Door of Hope: Recognizing and Resolving the Pains of Your Past.* San Bernardino: Here's Life Publishers, 1987.

Gil, Eliana. *Outgrowing the Pain: A Book for and about Adults Abused as Children.* New York: Deli Publishing, 1983.

Rush, Florence. *The Best Kept Secret: Sexual Abuse of Children.* New York: McGraw-Hill, 1980.

Development Issues

Kaplan, Louise J. *Oneness and Separateness: From Infant to Individual.* New York: Simon & Schuster, 1978.

General Recovery

Beattie, Melody. *Codependent No More: How to Stop Controlling Others and Start Caring for Yourself.* San Francisco: Harper/Hazelden, 1987.

Berry, Carmen Renee. *When Helping You Is Hurting Me: Escaping the Messiah Trap.* San Francisco: Harper & Row, 1988.

Bozarth-Campbell, Alla. *Life Is Goodbye, Life Is Hello: Grieving Well through All Kinds of Loss.* Minneapolis: CompCare Publishers, 1986.

Bradshaw, John. *Healing the Shame That Binds You.* Deerfield Beach, FL: Health Communications, 1988.

————. *The Family.* Deerfield Beach, FL: Health Communications, 1988.

Lerner, Harriet Goldhor. *The Dance of Anger: A Woman's Guide to Changing the Patterns of Intimate Relationships.* New York: Harper & Row, 1985.

Marlin, Emily. *Genograms: The New Tool for Exploring the Personality, Career, and Love Patterns You Inherit.* Chicago: Contemporary Books, 1989.

Mellody, Pia. *Facing Codependence: What It Is: Where It Comes From: How It Sabotages Our Lives.* San Francisco: Harper & Row, 1989.

Quinn, Valerie, *Professional Therapy Never Includes Sex*, Sacramento: Board of Behavioral Science Examiners, California Dept. of Consumer Affairs, 1990.

Siegel, Bernie S. *Love, Medicine, and Miracles: Lessons Learned about Self-Healing from a Surgeon's Experience with Exceptional Patients.* New York: Harper & Row, 1986.

Parenting the Inner Child

Pollard, John K. III. *Self-Parenting: The Complete Guide to Your Inner Conversations.* Malibu, CA: Generic Human Studies Publishing, 1987.

Reardon, Ruth. *Listening to the Littlest.* O. R. Gibson, 1989.

Whitfield, Charles. *Healing the Child Within.* Pompano Beach, FL: Health Communications, 1987.

Sexual Addiction

Carnes, Patrick. *Out of the Shadows: Understanding Sexual Addiction.* Minneapolis: CompCare, 1983.

Spirituality and Healing from Trauma

Buehler, Rich. *Rich and Pretending: You Can Be Set Free from the Hurts of the Past.* Nashville: Thomas Nelson, 1988.

Fortune, Marie M. *Keeping the Faith: Questions and Answers for the Abused Women.* San Francisco: Harper & Row, 1987.

Johnson, Robert A. *Inner Work.* San Francisco: Harper & Row, 1986.

Powell, John. *Why Am I Afraid to Tell You Who I Am?* Niles, IL: Argus Communications, 1969.

Seamands, David A. *Healing of Memories.* Wheaton, IL: Victor Books, 1985.

Smedes, Lewis. *Forgive and Forget: Healing the Hurts We Don't Deserve.* San Francisco: Harper & Row, 1984.

————. *How Can It Be All Right When Everything Is All Wrong?* San Francisco: Harper & Row, 1982.

Weems, Renita J. *Just A Sister Away: A Womanist Vision of Women's Relationships in the Bible.* San Diego: LuraMedia, 1988.

Yancey, Philip. *Disappointment with God: Three Questions No One Asks Aloud.* Grand Rapids, MI: Zondervan, 1988.

Resources for Clergy

Fortune, Marie. *Sexual Violence: The Unmentionable Sin.* New York: Pilgrim Press, 1983.

Horton, Anne L., and Williamson, Judith A. *Abuse and Religion— When Praying Isn't Enough.* Lexington, MA: Lexington Books, 1988.

Pellauer, Mary D.; Chester, Barbara; and Boyajian, Jane. *Sexual Assault and Abuse: A Manual for Clergy and Religious Professionals.* San Francisco: Harper & Row, 1987.

Self-Help and Support Group Resources

Adult Survivors of Child Sexual Abuse

Adults Molested As Children United
P.O. Box 952
San Jose, CA 95108
(408) 280-5055

Professionally led groups for survivors; this is a division of Parents United International.

VOICES—Victims of Incest Can Emerge Survivors
P.O. Box 148309
Chicago, IL 60614
(312) 327-1500

National network of survivor-led support groups for adults molested as children. Secular.

VIRTUES—Victims of Incest Recover Through Understanding Education, and Support
P.O. Box 602
Brea, CA 92622-0602

Professionally supervised Christian support groups in church and para-church group settings. Groups available for female survivors, and non-offending mothers of victims.

Alcohol and Drug Addiction

Alcoholics Anonymous World Services
P.O. Box 459, Grand Central Station
New York, NY 10163
(212) 686-110

Internationally acclaimed self-help program for recovering alcoholics.

Narcotics Anonymous
P.O. Box 9999
Van Nuys, CA 91409
(818) 780-3951

N.A. offers self-help groups for recovering drug addicts based on the 12-step A.A. program.

Overcomers' Outreach
2290 West Whittier Blvd.
La Habra, CA 90631
(213) 697-3994

Christian organization patterned after the Alcoholics Anonymous 12-step model. Deals with alcohol, drug, and food addiction, as well as codependency issues. Includes 600 chapters worldwide.

Eating Disorders

Overeaters Anonymous
2190 West 190th St.
Torrance, CA 90504
(213) 320-7941

Provides 12-step self-help groups for people with eating disorders.

Codependency

Al-Anon Family Group Headquarters
One Park Avenue
New York, NY 10016
(212) 683-1771

12-step self-help groups for husbands, wives and children of alcoholics.

Codependents of Sexual Addicts
P.O. Box 14537
Minneapolis, MN 55414

12-step self-help groups for husbands, wives and children of sexual addicts.

Families Anonymous (codependents of drug abusers)
P.O. Box 528
Van Nuys, CA 91408
(818) 989-7841

12-step self-help groups for husbands, wives and children of drug addicts.

Sexual Addiction

Sex Addicts Anonymous (SAA)
P.O. Box 3038
Minneapolis, MN 55403
(612) 339-0217

12-step self-help groups for recovering sex addicts.